Plainsong and Mediaeval Music Society

The elements of plainsong

Compiled from a series of lectures delivered before the members

Plainsong and Mediaeval Music Society

The elements of plainsong
Compiled from a series of lectures delivered before the members

ISBN/EAN: 9783337175801

Printed in Europe, USA, Canada, Australia, Japan

Cover: Foto ©Thomas Meinert / pixelio.de

More available books at **www.hansebooks.com**

THE

ELEMENTS OF PLAINSONG.

COMPILED FROM

A SERIES OF LECTURES

DELIVERED BEFORE THE MEMBERS OF THE

PLAINSONG & MEDIÆVAL MUSIC SOCIETY.

EDITED BY

H. B. BRIGGS.

——

POPULAR EDITION.

——

BERNARD QUARITCH, 15 PICCADILLY, LONDON, W.

1895.

LONDON :
—WATERLOW AND SONS LIMITED, PRINTERS, —
LONDON WALL, E.C.

CONTENTS.

		PAGE
PREFACE .	.	V
GENERAL OUTLINE	. *H. B. Briggs* .	1
TONALITY	. *Rev. W. Howard Frere* .	14
NOTATION	. *H. B. Briggs* .	22
RHYTHM .	. *C. F. Abdy Williams*	30
STRUCTURE	. *H. B. Briggs*	43
PSALMODY	. *Rev. G. H. Palmer*	54
HYMNODY	. *Rev. W. Howard Frere* .	68
MUSIC OF THE HOLY EUCHARIST	. *Rev. W. Howard Frere* .	79
ACCOMPANIMENT	. *Rev. W. Howard Frere* .	86
MUSICAL EXAMPLES : The Tonale . .	. .	(1)
Antiphons, etc. . .	.	(10)
Hymns	. .	(17)
Sequences	.	(21)
Part of a Gradual .	.	(26)

PREFACE.

THE religious revival of the past half-century was accompanied in its early years by the recognition of Plainsong as essentially the proper music for the Church's Services. It followed in this respect the intentions of Cranmer and the draughtsmen of Elizabeth's Injunctions, who, rejecting the florid harmonised Masses that had long been the fashion, expressly ordered Plainsong for Divine Service itself while admitting polyphonic music before or after it. It chanced that the Reformers, in thus ruling, unwittingly acted on their principle of appeal from the Mediæval to the Primitive Church, for Plainsong is undoubtedly the creation of the first six centuries of Christianity. With truly marvellous vitality it resisted corruption for at least seven hundred years, and only gradually succumbed to the influences which led to the religious reaction of the sixteenth century. Its revival is therefore in the truest sense a completion of the work of the Reformation, and should secure the support of Churchmen who may differ widely on other matters. To most musicians it opens up a new realm of art, and one which invariably fascinates all who have the enterprise to undertake the quest.

A perusal of the following pages will show that the plainsong which may be heard in most foreign churches is a mere parody of the art, and unfortunately it was from this source that our early Restorers were forced to draw their information. The researches of foreign *savants* had not by then advanced sufficiently to produce any effect on the prevailing ignorance, and English students were consequently obliged to rely on text books which have since been proved to be worthless. It was not until Dom Pothier, by the publication of *Les Melodies Grégoriennes* in 1880, applied to plainsong the methods of exact criticism which were originated in History by Ranke, that any certain basis was found for the revival of the art. While the fullest honour and gratitude must be given to the early workers in the field, we have therefore to regret that so much of their labour was misapplied, and that now the restoration of the use of plainsong has to contend not only with ignorance, but with prejudices due to its misrepresentation before the musical world.

The contents of this volume, consisting mainly of papers read before The Plainsong and Mediæval Music Society embody opinions for which, necessarily, the writers are themselves alone responsible, but they endeavour to present to English readers some outlines of the theory of plainsong set forth in the publications issued by the RR. PP. Benedictines of the Abbey of Solesmes, Sarthe, France. The conclusions on a few minor points may be matters of controversy, but with these exceptions they are those which have won the adhesion of the great majority of Continental students. Certain repetitions in the contents of the various chapters are unavoidable, but there is, perhaps, not much harm in this defect, as it may serve to enforce necessary truths.

Besides *Les Mélodies Grégoriennes* the Solesmes Fathers have published three volumes of *facsimiles* of MSS. (*Paléographie Musicale*, Solesmes, 1889, etc.,) with Introductions showing a theory of plainsong deduced from internal evidence, and editions of the Service Books with the chant copied from the MSS. and consequently very different from other versions issued during this century, especially those of Mechlin and Ratisbon. The latter is a mere reprint of the Medicean and Lichtenstein editions of the 16th century (which scarcely pretend to reproduce the chant as it is found with practical uniformity in the MSS. of the preceding six centuries), and its extreme inaccuracy will be perceived on comparing it with the melodies here printed which are extracted from MSS. In addition to the above works there may be recommended to students *Etude sur le Chant Grégorien*, (Thiery 1886,) *Théorie et pratique du Chant Grégorien*, (Kienle, 1888,) *Rhythme, Exécution, et Accompagnement du Chant Grégorien*, (Lhoumeau, 1892,) all published by Desclée Lefebvre et Cie. Tournai, and the *Revue du Chant Grégorien*, a monthly publication inspired from Solesmes. For original research there are also available the ancient treatises reprinted by Gerbert in *Scriptores Ecclesiastici de Musica Sacra*, 1774, and by Coussemaker in *Scriptores de Musica Medii Ævi*, 1876. Of works in English, a great deal of information can be found in the translation of the Ratisbon *Magister Choralis*, Walker's *Plainsong Reason Why*, and Helmore's *Primer of Plainsong*, but as these were written before the Solesmes Fathers had published the result of their researches, considerable discrimination is required in the reader.

For detailed information on the History of Hymnody the reader is referred to Lord Selborne's *Hymns* (A. & C. Black 1892) and to Julian's

Dictionary of Hymnology (Murray 1892). References in the paper on Hymnody are made to the following collections of plainsong melodies :—

    1. P.H.M.—Plainsong Hymn Melodies (at the office of "The Organist and Choirmaster") (in the press).

    2. H.N.—The Hymnal Noted (Novello).

    3. O.H.B.—The Office Hymn Book (Pickering & Chatto).

    4. P.M.—The Plainsong Melodies of "Hymns Ancient and Modern" (Masters).

The Latin original texts are to be found best in the collections of Daniel, *Thesaurus Hymnologicus*, Mone, *Lateinische Hymnen*, Kehrein, *Lateinische Sequenzen*, Dreves, *Analecta Hymnica*, Misset & Weale, *Analecta Liturgica.*

For Sequences special reference should be made to Léon Gautier's *Œuvres poétiques d'Adam de St. Victor* (Paris 1858) and to his *Histoire de la poésie liturgique au moyen age*, t. i. *Les Tropes* (Paris 1886), and to *The Winchester Troper* (Henry Bradshaw Society 1894).

The pages of Examples relating to the Tones and their pointing (pp. (1) to (9)) are extracted, by permission, from the *Sarum Psalter* (Geo. Bell & Sons).

GENERAL OUTLINE.

PLAINSONG or *Cantus planus*—even, level, plain song—is perfectly distinct from *cantus figuratus*, or *mensuratus*, *i.e.* harmonised, measured music, from which it essentially differs in tonality and rhythm. It is true that for a time measured music was affected by the *tonality* of plainsong, but never by the *rhythm*, which is the more important part. No well-informed musician, in comparing the two systems, can therefore claim that the one is merely a barbarous and undeveloped form of the other, and unworthy of attention except on antiquarian grounds.

In spite of a revival of disputes about the tradition, it is practically certain that the bulk of the music comprised under the term plainsong, as it exists in MSS. or in the printed Solesmes Editions, was put into its present form by S. Gregory the Great about A.D. 600. The MSS., moreover, which give the Ambrosian Chant, show us a system of music which is essentially the same as the Gregorian, and often in a more florid form, so that plainsong is thus carried back to the Fourth century. Beyond that we can only guess as to its origin.

Its two leading characteristics may be shortly described as follows: Whereas modern music recognises only two scales, viz. the major and minor, plainsong contains eight, strictly diatonic but all differing in the relative positions of their intervals to the keynote. In measured music moreover the rhythm is *fixed*, *i.e.* the accents are at regular fixed periods of time. In plainsong the accents occur irregularly, thus making the rhythm *free*, but subject to certain laws of proportion which satisfy the ear. Measured music is there-

fore strictly applicable to the fixed rhythm of poetry, and
plainsong is more suitable for the free rhythm of prose.

TONALITY.—The scales or *modes* used in plainsong are
the octaves beginning on every note in the natural scale
A B C D E F G. The original or *authentic* modes were those
starting from D E F and G, and to these, in order to increase
their compass, were added their *plagals* which are the octa-
chords on the fourths below, viz., A B C and D. The authentic
and its corresponding plagal could be used in the same composition, the finals of both being identical. Other modes are
only transpositions of these eight by means of the insertion
of B♭, which is allowable although no other chromatic notes
are admitted into this strictly diatonic system. In an untrans-
posed mode the B♭ is also allowed as an accidental for the
purpose of avoiding a tritone between B and F. Every melody
ends on the keynote of the mode in which it is written—hence
called the *final*. In each mode there is a certain note called
the *dominant*, but not necessarily the fifth from the final, which
recurs frequently in a melody, and is in fact the reciting note
round which circle all others even in the most elaborate Chants.

It will be seen from the Table that the modes were con-
structed by the juxtaposition of two tetrachords taken from
the original Great Scale of A, and the varied positions of the
semitones in relation to the finals give each mode a distinctive
character of its own not to be found in the transpositions of
the two modern scales. In Byzantine music combinations of
diatonic tetrachords produce thirty-six scales, while combinations of chromatic tetrachords give two hundred and fifty-three
scales all differing from each other.[1] The Gregorian modes
however are simply octaves out of the Greek diatonic scale,
and, though bearing the Greek names, are not the same as the
later Greek scales, but descended from them to the West in
an altered form through the mathematician Boethius. (d. 526
A.D.) The theoretical treatises extant are few, but we find that

---

[1] See *Byzantine Music*, S. G. Hatherly (Alex. Gardner).

the earliest writers regarded the modes more as combinations of
tetrachords than as octaves ; that in the 10th century musical
theory began to be emancipated from its old fetters and to
join hands with practical music, and there grew up a recognition of the intimate relation of the final and its fifth ; and

TABLE OF MODES.

Mode.	Character.	Range.	Final.	Dominant.	
I. Dorian	Authentic	D E F G A B C D	D	A	Regular Modes.
II. Hypodorian	Plagal	A B C D E F G A		F	
III. Phrygian	Authentic	E F G A B C D E	E	C	
IV. Hypophrygian	Plagal	B C D E F G A B		A	
V. Lydian	Authentic	F G A B C D E F	F	C	
VI. Hypolydian	Plagal	C D E F G A B C		A	
VII. Mixolydian	Authentic	G A B C D E F G	G	D	
VIII. Hypomixolydian	Plagal	D E F G A B C D		C	
IX. Æolian	Authentic	A B C D E F G A	A	E	Transposed Modes.
X. Hypozolian	Plagal	E F G A B C D E		C	
XI. Locrian	Authentic	B C D E F G A B	B	G	
XII. Hypolocrian	Plagal	F G A B C D E F		E	
XIII. Ionian	Authentic	C D E F G A B C	C	G	
XIV. Hypoionian	Plagal	G A B C D E F G		E	

that in the 11th century the adoption of Guido's hexa-
chordal solmisation of the gamut paved the way for the
complete recognition by the theorists of the octachordal
system.

The *dominant* in an authentic mode is the first note of
the upper tetrachord, and in the corresponding plagal the
third below the authentic dominant, but in the 3rd and 8th
modes it is changed in order to avoid falling on B, which was
liable to be flattened. In the 11th mode, which corresponds
to the 3rd, the dominant is also moved from the doubtful F to
G. But analysis of melodies shows not infrequent exceptions
to the rule of the prevalence of the supposed dominant of
the mode in which the chant, judging from its final, is written,
and the whole subject of tonality awaits further research.

The purest melodies do not exceed the compass of their
mode by more than one or two notes, but later compositions
of the 11th century and onwards frequently overpass it.

NOTATION.—The first efforts of musicians to delineate
in writing the sounds of the gamut were necessarily very tentative. The Greeks had a complete system of notation, but for
some reason it was not used by the early Church musicians, who
started afresh on other lines. The gradual development of
plainsong and its frequent repetition, with consequent oral trans-
mission, among the clerics of great churches, doubtless led to
the system which we find in MSS. of the ninth or tenth century,
which are the earliest extant. It was formed by the use of
the acute (′) and grave (`) accents, showing when the voice as-
cended or descended, and combinations of these accents formed
neums, or notegroups, which were to be sung at a single effort of
the voice, and corresponded *somewhat* to a modern bar. These
signs, which are also called *neums*, consequently showed neither
tonal nor time-value, but served well as a reminder of the chant
that was already known by ear. In the eleventh century in
order to fix their tonal value they were put on a staff of four
lines, which with a moveable C **C**, F **∱**, or B♭ **♭** clef, was
amply sufficient for a melody in unison.[1] But they still
indicated no time-value; this was a development of the

---

[1] All the letters of the gamut were at times used as clefs.

twelfth century, when the practice of harmony led to the adoption, with a fixed time-value, of the three forms of notes with which the chances of caligraphy had endowed plainsong notation. It is however evident from the MSS. that the time-values of *longs*, *breves*, and *semibreves*, had nothing to do with plainsong, so that sixteenth century writers, such as Merbecke, only described the debased notation of their own century in making a lozenge equal to half a square note, and that again equal to half a tailed note. As a matter of fact, the early harmonists made each note equal three of the next lesser denomination, but knew perfectly well that in the Church MSS. the shapes of the notes depended solely on their neumatic origin, or the handwriting of the scribe. The notes on a plainsong staff therefore simply indicate the relative pitch of the sounds *without any time-value*. The clef indicates the line or space on which C, F, or B♭ falls, and other intervals are reckoned from it. Transposition is therefore perfectly easy as **C** indicates the keynote, **𝄐** the fourth, and **b** the minor seventh of the scale into which it is desired to transpose the chant. The ♭ when interpolated is not continued beyond the neum in which it occurs. When two notes are placed together thus, **▮** it is the lower which is first sounded, when thus, **𝄐■** the upper note is first sung. The long stroke in **◥** indicates two notes, viz., those on the space or line on which the stroke begins and ends. To these two this neum adds a third, which is higher than the second of the two notes shown by the stroke.

Bars are used to show the end of phrases which are technically called *distinctions*. A half bar across the staff means a breathmark, a whole bar quite across the staff a *pause* with a *rallentando*, and a double bar a still longer pause and *rallentando*. A guide ⌇ shows the position of the next note after the end of a staff or when the clef is changed.

RHYTHM.—We come now to the consideration of *rhythm*, which is the most important element in plainsong,

The rhythm of modern music was not derived from that of plainsong, but primarily from that of the dance-songs of Northern Europe. The mediæval *cantus mensuratus* or *figuratus*, in which the individual notes were *measured*, partook neither of the rhythm of ancient plainsong, nor of that of modern music; for that essential feature of all rhythm, the *phrase*, was either entirely absent from it, or only vaguely indicated.

The construction of the *cantus figuratus* of Palestrina's epoch is perhaps best described in the following passage from Richard Wagner's " Beethoven " :

" Here (*i.e.* in Palestrina's music) the rhythmus is only " perceptible through the interchange of chord successions, " while it does not exist as symmetrical divisions of time. " The time-divisions are so intimately bound up with the " essence of harmony, which, in itself, is timeless, that the " laws of time are of no assistance for understanding this kind " of music. The single time-division only shows itself as the " most delicate variation of a primary harmonic colour, which " is displayed to us through the most varied progressions, " without our being able to perceive any sign of fixed lines in " the changes. And since this harmonic colour is not con- " tained in a given space of time, we obtain, as it were, a " timeless and spaceless picture, an entirely spiritual revela- " tion, through which we are affected with indescribable " emotion, since it represents to us more clearly than " anything else, the inmost essence of religion, free from all " dogmatic ideas."

In modern music, accents occur at regular intervals of time, forming two-time and three-time measures, which correspond with the feet of verse. A combination of several measures forms a *colon* or *phrase*, corresponding with a single line in a stanza, while two or more cola form a *period*, answering to a couplet. Modern music requires that these feet and cola should be combined strictly according to rule, exactly as feet and lines are combined in poetry. Apparent irregularities occur in the musical form, just as they do in a poem, but they are irregular only to a casual observer; a closer analysis shows that there is strict order in the seeming disorder. And besides this absolute regularity of form in the greater divisions of notes, there is a mathematical precision of time-value amongst the notes themselves. There may be *rallentandos* or *accelerandos*, but the even tenor of a composition is not thereby disturbed, and notes of the same denomination have essentially always an equal value. Without this precision part-singing would be impossible.

The rhythm of plainsong is founded on a different system. We are at once confronted with the fact that the Offices of the Church are not in poetry but in prose. Consequently the accents, whether in the Latin or English text, occur quite irregularly as compared with those in a poem. The modern composer generally fits his prose text to the musical form by a necessary disregard of the time-value of syllables, and lengthens or shortens them at will. The original church-musicians however adopted another system, viz., that the text was the chief consideration, and that in place of the words being subordinate to the music, the music was to illustrate the words, the chant even being in places specially adapted to the due pronunciation of every syllable.

The merit of good prose consists in its rhythm as much as in the choice of expressive phrases, and the rhythm of a great orator depends on the proportionate succession of accents in his sentences. An analysis of these will show that a certain balance is preserved amongst them, so that a sentence containing five accented syllables will be followed by one with three, or seven accents may be opposed to five, and so on. Greater proportions rarely occur, *e.g.* a phrase with seven or eight accents seldom answers to one in which there are only two or three. Every Latin word contains only one tonic accent, and as groups of short words in English fairly represent the longer words of Latin, the same laws are applicable to both languages, and the same balance is preserved among sentences. For instance *Glóry be to Gód on hígh* contains three accents, while *and on eárth peáce, goodwíll towards men* has four. The whole of the text of our services may be thus analysed with the same results, and in its finer developments the laws of the *cursus*, as it is called, can be reduced to such precision that in the old Latin collects it is possible to tell from it the dates at which they were written. This variable, though essential proportion of accented syllables constitutes the free rhythm of prose in contradistinction to the fixed rhythm of poetry and its accompanying metrical music. It is therefore evident that, given the text with its free oratorical rhythm, the music should follow the same system.

STRUCTURE.—Chanting undoubtedly developed from the necessity that everyone finds when speaking in the open air, or in a large building, for adopting certain conventionalities of pitch which are needless in ordinary conversation. This need not be particularly enforced ; it may be heard in street cries, in the old fashioned reading, or rather preaching the prayers, and specially in Welsh preaching, where a very decided and regular series of inflections is introduced at emphatic parts of the sermon. This is the origin of plainsong. We have it still in its simplest form in the Versicles and Responses, and rather more elaborately in the Cantus of the Epistles and Gospels, the Prefaces etc. If the distinction may be allowed, the result is chanting not singing. It is the recitation on one or more definite notes of the text that would otherwise be said with all the infinite gradations of tone of ordinary speech ; but the accentuation of the text is not in any way changed, nor the syllables given any fixed proportionate time-value. Thus, if the Versicles and Responses be properly rendered, the Priest and People will answer each other in chants which flow easily along their reciting notes and inflections with a perpetually varying time-value to the syllables. But if sung to Tallis' harmonies for instance, the natural accentuation tends to be quite destroyed in the people's Response, and the free rhythm is stretched out on the Procrustean bed of fixed accents and mathematical time. The artistic sense must be considerably deadened by custom before it can endure the excruciating effect of this corrupted rendering in alternation with the free rhythm of the Priest's part.

There is much more in these simple Responses than at first sight appears. Merbecke in his longer adaptations and compositions lost the spirit of genuine plainsong, but as regards the simpler ritual music, which had been purer in its traditions, he proved more trustworthy. The Latin rule for the shortened mediations in the 2nd, 5th, and 8th Tones, which means ending them on the rising note, is that they should be used for all monosyllables and Hebrew words. Modern Psalter-makers object to this, because, they say, it gives too much prominence to such words as *be* or *me*, not grasping the fact that, as the music has no fixed accent, the undue emphasis is given only by bad and loud singing which should be corrected. But in the Responses, as well as in his settings of the Tones, we find that Merbecke adhered to the Latin rule, and that his ear felt nothing faulty in it. Where there is a word of two or more syllables at the end of the sentence, the last reciting note is allotted to the accented syllable, and the remainder of the word

F F F D
is sung to a minor third below, as . . . . . *thy salvation* . . . . .
F D D
righteousness. But when the last word is a monosyllable the
F D E F
music rises a tone, as . . . . . *save the Queen* . . . . . *call*
F D E
upon thee. Here it will be noticed that in the former the D is unaccented, but in the latter it carries an accent, and the E has only the due prominence which belongs to the word. If sung without accompaniment an even rendering is easily obtained, and there will be no gabble on the reciting note with a pause before the inflection such as is often heard in *And make thy chosen people ‖ joyful.* There should of course be no break at all in the continuity of a sentence when sung either by priest or choir.

We now come to a slightly more elaborate form of plainsong than the ritual inflections. The simplest forms of the
Tones are the Ambrosian, which have no *mediations*, while
the *endings* rarely exceed the compass of the tetrachord, and
are syllabic except where the last note is converted into two.
The Gregorian Tones are more florid and always have a
mediation, while the compass extends to a Fifth; except in
the *Tonus Peregrinus* the reciting note is the same in both
halves of the Tone. The Tones have also *intonations*, which
are a few notes at the beginning to fix the melody in its proper
tetrachord. The leading principle therefore of a Gregorian
Psalm Tone is that it should have an intonation, a reciting note,
and a melodic inflection. These characteristics are preserved
in all pure plainsong, even in the most elaborate music, and the
absence of them, especially of the reciting note, in Merbecke's
and Dumont's Masses, makes these works very faulty examples.

The difference between the Tones and Anglican Chants
consists not only in tonality and the use of harmony, but in
the treatment of the inflections at the mediation and ending.
In Anglican Chants these are regular melodies in fixed
rhythm, allowing of no variability of accent, and requiring that
the words should be strictly adjusted to them according to the
time-value of the notes. Even the syllables sung to the
reciting note have to submit to the bondage of the metronome,
though, if treated rightly, the Anglican Chant would be the
connecting link between free and fixed rhythm. In the
Tones the music is subservient to the words, and, subject to
rallentandos, the notes sung to each syllable of a Psalm verse
have exactly the same time-value and accentuation as if the
Psalms were said in monotone. This gives a simplicity and
breadth to the chanting unattainable with fixed rhythm, and
the variability of accent avoids the monotony produced by
repetition of the short harmonized melody of a single Anglican
Chant, from which refuge is vainly sought in Double, nay even
Triple and Quadruple. Chants. The Psalms moreover are not
intended to be sung to elaborate services, but to be recited

simply and devotionally, so that the only form in which this
can be done really artistically is by the use of the Tones.
Unfortunately these have not hitherto been presented to
English congregations in their complete beauty, but the
learned researches of the Benedictines of Solesmes during the
last twenty years have thrown such light on their structure,
that what was before impossible has now been accomplished.*
Every Tone has only one mediation but various endings, which
were used for the purpose of passing gracefully to the first
note of the Antiphon, which rounded off the Tone by closing
on the final of the mode. Unless this is done either vocally
by the Antiphon, or instrumentally by the accompanist, the
effect is as faulty as that of a modern melody ending with
an unresolved discord.

The following specimens of pointing endings of the First
and Fourth Tones will show the variation of accent which
is produced by a right rendering of the Tones:—*Lord with*
hóly worship,—and feáthered fowls—imágine a vain thing—
together in unity. Lord with hóly worship—imágine a vain
thing—of all thy márvellous works. In every case it must
be observed that each note in itself has no accent except that
of the word, but that there is a *rallentando* on the last note,
or note-group, but one of the ending. The last note of the
mediation and ending should be sung *pianissimo* and *sostenuto*.
Great care should be taken to make no hiatus between the
reciting note and the inflections, and the words all through a
verse should be taken at the same rate, thus avoiding a gabble
on the reciting note and a fixed rhythm in the inflections.
The result will be that the chanting of the Psalms will sound
more like *reading* than *singing.* There should be a pause at
the colon, according to an old rule, long enough to say *Ave
Maria.*

The melodies of Antiphons are generally the simplest
form of the more florid or *melismatic* chant, which reaches its

---

* The *Sarum Psalter* (Geo. Bell & Sons, London).

greatest elaboration in Kyries, Graduals, and Offertories. These compositions are of the greatest beauty, and require no mean power of execution, though the necessary farsing in English of the Kyries reduces these to comparative simplicity of execution. The rest of the Ordinary of the Mass is of a more congregational character and can be easily sung by the people, the Creed especially being almost as simple in structure as a Psalm Tone. For this species of plain-song the only rule for a good execution is to learn the chant thoroughly, and, paying special attention to the accented syllables, pass quickly from one to the other of them, making good pauses at the end of sentences. The Church's Chant in fact provides that those portions of the service in which it is the people's duty to join with voice as well as heart shall be of easy execution, while others, of which the music is of a subjective character can only be rendered by trained singers.

The melodies to hymns, though in the old tonality, form a species by themselves more nearly akin to modern music. The ordinary metres in use imply a certain amount of time-value in the phrases, though, as the singing is unisonous, there is not the rigid fixed rhythm necessitated by the harmonies of modern hymns, but the free rhythm of a ballad, and the time-value of the note or neum on a syllable is regulated by the importance of that syllable in the metre of the verse.

With the exception of the hymn melodies, the various forms of plainsong, viz., the *syllabic*, as in the Creed, and the *melismatic* as in a Gradual, all contain the same vital principle of the free rhythm of prose, as opposed to the fixed rhythm of poetry and modern music. The problem of treating melodically a prose text has therefore been artistically solved in plainsong, and in that system alone. In its simpler forms it is suited to the capabilities of the ordinary village choir, and the less organ accompaniment there is the better. In its more ornate examples it taxes the powers of the best trained vocalists, and unless rendered by a choir so composed, it cannot be expected to produce its full effect, so that any

comparison of it under adverse conditions with trained perform-
ances of modern music is manifestly unfair. Moreover, as
plainsong is a perfectly unknown art to most people, musical
critics, who are mindful of the conflicts of taste over any new
form of modern music, will abstain from expressing an opinion
on its æsthetic merits, until they have by some study and
experience acquainted themselves with its theory and practice.

TONALITY.

There is a difference of character between ancient ecclesi-astical music and modern music which is very obvious, and is easily felt by many who would be at a loss to know exactly how to analyse and describe it ; this difference rests on two points in which early music and modern music are sharply contrasted, viz., rhythm and tonality.

It is with the latter that we are concerned here, and it may be as well to begin at once with a definition.

The tonality of a scale, mode, or melody is that peculiar flavour which attaches to it, and is derived from the mutual relationship of the notes which compose it.

For every musical purpose a certain selection is made out of the infinite variety of possible sounds, and it is as the result of a long evolution that western music now possesses the chromatic scale—the division of the octave into twelve semitones—and the diatonic scale in which the same interval is divided into 7 degrees consisting of five tones and two semi-tones arranged in a continuous series thus :—

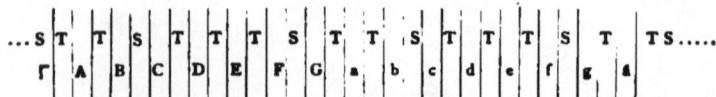

...S T T S T T T S T T S T T T S T TS.....
Γ A B C D E F G a b c d e f g a

Ancient ecclesiastical music confines itself almost entirely to the diatonic scale ; it is therefore the above series of notes which we have to investigate, and the question is, how are we to catch and define so intangible a thing as tonality—a musical flavour.

Theoretically every collection of notes has a flavour or tonality which is quite peculiar to itself ; but for prac-tical purposes melodies can be classified by certain main characteristics.

The tonality springs *from the mutual relationship of the notes*, and this mutual relationship expresses itself most clearly in three particulars.

1. We must take into account the actual notes employed : that is the *range* of the melody.

2. We must see how it ends ; for it is essential that a melody should lead up to and leave off on a note which can be considered as *final*.

3. Since early melody is all more or less developed from monotonic recitative with inflections, we may expect to find one note more prominent than the rest, and round which the others circle, which may therefore be called the *dominant* note.

These three points will give some very clear insight into the mutual relationship of the notes of a melody, that is into its tonality.

It is customary to divide plainsong melodies according to their tonality into eight classes, or *modes*, each of which has a clearly fixed (i) range, (ii) final, and (iii) dominant.

1. For ordinary purposes an octave is quite sufficient range for any one melody ; formerly indeed a pentachord or even a tetrachord was considered a sufficient unit of range, and it is convenient even now to look upon the normal octave of a plainsong mode as composed of a pentachord and a tetrachord which coalesce, thus :—

```
A B C D                    D E F G a
      D E F G a    or               a b c d
```

These eight modes, considered as containing an octave each, comprise the whole range of the diatonic scale from A (that is the bottom space of the bass clef) to g, nearly two octaves above it ; but practically the several modes are not limited to a bare octave, nor is the range of the diatonic scale limited to two octaves. It was found necessary to recognise a note below the low A, to which was given the name of Γ, *gamma*, (hence the term *gamut* for the scale,) while the upward range was extended to a', and even higher notes occur where a melody has been transposed.

2. For this system of eight modes four notes are employed
as finals, viz., D E F G : each one has a pair of modes connected with it ; the first of the pair is called an authentic
mode, and in it the pentachord is below the tetrachord
thus :—

D E F G a
    a b c d :

the other is called a plagal mode and in it the tetrachord is
below the pentachord thus :—

A B C D
    D E F G a :

and the final is in one case the lowest note of the scale but
in the other case the central note of it.

3. The dominant note in an authentic mode is the fifth
or central note, and the dominant of a plagal mode is a third
below the dominant of the corresponding authentic ·mode :
but b♮ came to be considered not a sufficiently stable note
to be a dominant, and c was substituted in its place.

The following table sums up the various modes : the
asterisk marks the final and the obelus the dominant :

1st.				D*	E	F	G	a†	b	c	d		
2nd.	A	B	C	D*	E	F†	G	a					
3rd.					E*	F	G	a	b	c†	d	e	
4th.		B	C	D	E*	F	G	a†	b				
5th.						F*	G	a	b	c†	d	e	f
6th.			C	D	E	F*	G	a†	b	c			
7th.							G*	a	b	c	d†	e	f	g
8th.				D	E	F	G*	a	b	c†	d		

These eight types are sufficiently comprehensive to include
nearly all the Gregorian melodies ; for the rigidity of the
modal system was considerably lessened when the theorists
found themselves obliged to recognise the use of b♭, which
occurs constantly in the old melodies, partly to obtain a
special effect, and partly to avoid the harshness of the tritone,
or interval from F to b♮. Moreover, with this liberty granted,
it is unnecessary to reckon more than these eight, for the so-
called 9th—14th modes, recognised by some later theorists,
which have a, b, c as their finals, are the same as the first six
modes, only transposed a fifth higher.

So the eight ecclesiastical modes stand out as the types of eight different sorts of melodies broadly distinguished by their range, their dominant, and their final.

But the student must not be content with this, which is after all only a very rough and ready estimate of tonality ; therefore we must proceed to a more minute study of the several modes.

We have hitherto ignored the modern scales, but now, having defined the ancient scales, it is worth while to come down to modern times and take them into consideration, using them as standards of comparison ; for we are all nowadays so infected with the tonality of the modern scales that the simplest way for us (though not in itself the best way) to distinguish any other tonality, is by contrasting the unfamiliar mode with one or other of those with which we are more familiar.

While the ancients used eight modes, modern music only uses two, the major and the minor mode, and the latter in a very variable form ; neither of the modern ones forms part of the old system but they are sufficiently like to be most valuable for purposes of comparison.

Every one is familiar with the difference of tonality between the major and the minor mode : when analysed it is found to depend on two places in the scale—the third, and the sixth and seventh.

Taking the following series of notes and intervals—

```
T  T  S  T  T  S  T  T  T  S  T  T  S  T  T
Γ  A  B  C  D  E  F  G  a  b  c  d  e  f  g  á
```

the major mode may be represented thus T T S T T T S while the minor mode begins T S T T and then leaves the diatonic scale altogether : a simple comparison such as this is very helpful in distinguishing the tonality of major and minor.

Similarly it is possible to take each of the old modes and compare it with one or other of the modern scales, note the one or two crucial spots in it, and so by contrast elicit a good

c

deal as to its tonality. We begin with the first; its formula
is T S T T T S T or in other words its semitones come in
the second and sixth places: the first mode then is very like
the minor scale (of D) ; when the b is flattened, as is often
the case, the similarity is closer still, and the thing which
most distinguishes it from the modern use of the minor is the
flat seventh or absence of leading note. The crucial spots in
the scale are then the sixth and seventh ; but as a matter of
fact the greater part of first-mode melodies are to a great
extent concerned with the lower pentachord of the mode
between the final and the dominant ; if they rise to the sixth
it is usually flattened ; less frequently the melody ascends to
the seventh or octave, and then in descending the b♮ is often
kept. (¹) The flat seventh is however a marked characteristic
of this mode since it constantly appears *below* the final.
Page (16) gives the eight typical melodies written to serve
as specimens of the different tonalities of the eight modes;
it will be observed that ex. i only once ascends to the bb,
and that in a typical opening phrase, which constantly recurs
in melodies of the first mode.

The melodies of the second mode are of much the same
minor character, and usually their range is even more
restricted (p. (16), ex. ii); they generally keep within the
limits of the octave but if they rise above a they flatten the b.

The note B is generally avoided ; sometimes when Bb is
wanted the whole melody is transposed a fifth higher, and the
effect is then obtained by the F♮ ; a similar transposition
sometimes takes place when there is no B at all (p. (19), ex. 9).
The well-known Advent Antiphons called the Greater O's
are fine examples of florid melodies in this mode.(²)

The formula of the third mode in S T T T S T T : the
semitone E F, as the first interval, is the most remarkable

---

(1) A fine instance of a *pure* first mode melody without b b anywhere is
that of *Aeterne Christe* P.H.M. 46. Compare *Ave Maris Stella* P.H.M. 63.

(2) See *The Antiphons to Magnificat throughout the Year* (Geo. Bell & Sons
1894) which contains these and the other Sarum Antiphons to *Magnificat* adapted
to English words.

feature here and gives a very definite character to the mode ; but the larger part of most third mode melodies range round the dominant c, and often the true tonality only becomes unmistakeable on descending to the final at the end of the melody ; in other cases the occurrence of a plain and comprehensive third mode figure (such as the opening phrase of the neupma in p. (16), ex. iii) betrays the tonality at once. Occasionally when F♯ is wanted the whole melody is transposed a fourth higher and the required effect is then obtained by b♮ while b♭ can be still used as representing F♮ ; a well-known instance of this is the Sarum form of the hymn-melody *Pange lingua*.([1])

In the fourth mode the semitone interval above the final still remains the chief characteristic, and this becomes even more marked here because the melodies to a great extent range round the final, instead of, as in the third mode, round the dominant ; their compass is often very small.

The natural result of this is the constant use of F and consequently a tendency to flatten the B or b so as to avoid a tritone. The b is easily flattened by the simple insertion of ♭ ; when it is the lower B that is to be flattened, the effect is obtained, as in the case of the second mode, by transposing the melody a fifth higher, when F♮ represents the B♭.

Another phase of the fourth mode must be touched upon because though peculiar it is of common occurrence. There is a whole series of antiphons in the Divine Office built upon one type of melody, of which *Benedicta tu* is probably the best known example. Here a deliberate step was taken, as in the 3rd mode, to avoid the F above the final, *i e.* the characteristic semitone : the melodies have all been transposed a fourth higher ; the note a then becomes the final ; it has a whole tone above it, but if the strict tonality of the fourth mode is required it can still be had (and is in fact employed in some of the series of antiphons) by using b♭.

---

(1) See P.H.M. No. 36.

C 2

But though in some melodies modifications such as these are made by flattening the fifth or sharpening the second of the mode, a very large proportion keep to the strict tonality. Page (16), ex. iv shews the main characteristics and the restricted range; other specimens may be seen in the hymn tunes Nos. 5, 6 and 15 on pp. (18) and (20).

The fifth and sixth modes present the closest affinity to the major scale, as they differ from it only in having normally the b♮. In the sixth mode this is constantly flattened, and then the difference is more apparent than real; in the fifth mode the older melodies generally keep the b♮, especially in descending, but it is often flattened in the later melodies. Again, these are the only modes which possess a leading note —a thing which may very easily lend itself to give a modern flavour—and besides they have of course the power of using their b♮ when convenient to lead up to c, thus giving something of the modern effect of a full close in the dominant. With all these modern possibilities in the hands of modern writers the fifth and sixth modes would have become identical with the major scale: in the hands of the old musicians they were saved from this apparently by the deliberate policy of the writers, who were slow to flatten the b unless it was absolutely necessary, and avoided as far as possible the modern use of the leading note (see p. (20) No. 16 and the typical melodies p. (16) ex. v and vi). The use of this pair of modes— the fifth especially—is far more restricted than that of others.

The principal characteristic of the seventh mode is its flat seventh; in other respects it is the key of G major. But often the F or f is a very prominent note in a seventh mode melody, and its tonality is in consequence quite clearly defined (page (16), ex. vii).

In the eighth mode it is again the same F that is distinctive, and differentiates the mode from the scale of G major. Sometimes as in p. (19), No. 11, there is no F and so far as the bare melody goes it might actually belong to the key of G: but this is no justification for treating the melody in harmonizing it as though it were in G major. The harmonies usually employed with the hymn tune quoted entirely destroy its character.

In p. (18) No. 8 and also in p. (20) No. 14 there is an instance of the growing tendency to flatten the b in the eighth mode ; it was a natural and perhaps inevitable tendency owing to the growing dislike to the tritone, but it spoilt the pure tonality. In cases where the ♭ was merely an obvious accidental the harm was not great and the gain to some tender ears considerable ; but as it became more and more common, it led on to the breaking down of the distinctions between modes, and to that general weakening of tonality which led the way to the modern poverty-stricken system of having only two modes.

In conclusion it is probably necessary to say a word to dispel the usual prejudices against the tonalities of the modal system. The ordinary musical public, and especially professional musicians in this country, are accustomed to put the whole thing on one side with the sublime contempt which springs from ignorance. It is so much easier to condemn the system as 'barbarous' than to take the trouble to find out what it means. But for anyone who will take this trouble there is an ample reward, for as the modal system unfolds itself before him he will discover whole mines of melodic treasure whose existence he never suspected before. Modern music has deliberately given these up so as to better exploit the veins of harmonic wealth which underlie the modern scales. No one need quarrel with this action, for the gain harmonically is immeasurable; but nevertheless the harmonic gain involved a melodic loss. So far as pure melody is concerned, there is infinitely more richness and variety in the old eight modes than in the two modern ones. A modern ear is often so warped and stunted that it fails to appreciate the beauties at first ; they are too new and strange for its limited and narrowed appreciation ; but that soon alters, and before long the old melodies with their peculiar tonality and severe harmonies, begin to exercise a fascination which, in its way, is quite as powerful as the gorgeous glory of modern harmony, and is much more suitable to serve religious ends.

NOTATION.

The earliest extant notation of Plainsong served only to remind singers of the melodies they had already learned by ear. It is termed the *neumatic* system from the *neums* or signs used, which do not show the tonal-value of the notes, but simply that one note is higher or lower than that immediately before or after it, and that the notes are grouped on a syllable in a certain manner. The term *neum* being first applied to the signs, whether of single or grouped notes, is also given to the *note-groups* in the later square notation. The original neums were the acute (*∕*) and grave (*∖*) accents of the grammarians, the former signifying an elevation of the voice, or a relatively high note, and the latter a depression of the voice, or a low note. Combinations of these accents formed note-groups to be sung at one effort of the voice, and a series of these formed a *distinction* or phrase. The grave accent was in time corrupted in many cases into a dot or a horizontal stroke, but in others retained its original form as in the *podatus* and *clivis*. The acute accent always retained its characteristic of an upward stroke, and this survives in the tailed-notes of the square notation. The accompanying Table of the neums in most general use will serve to explain the system ; as it only shows that there is *some* difference in pitch, but not what the difference is between two successive notes in a neum, it will be observed that the same symbol may represent notes at any interval apart.

Attempts were made in the ninth and tenth centuries, or perhaps earlier, to employ other systems of notation, such as writing the words on the spaces of a great staff, or placing the letters of the gamut over the words ; but these methods were apparently only used in practice for instruction-books or for early examples of harmony. The melodies being transmitted orally, the *memoria technica* provided by the neumatic notation practically answered all requirements, and was in some ways more explicit than the square notation, which was developed from it in the 11th century by placing the neums on a staff. This notation shows definitely the tonal intervals and the grouping of the notes, but misses the finer delicacies of phrasing, especially those which are shown in some forms of the neums, *e.g.* where the *Romanian Letters* have been added to serve as marks of expression and *tempo*, such as *c* for *celeriter*, *t* for *tene*, *f* for *fortiter* etc. In some MSS. there are *small strokes* across the heads of several neums, and these serve as signs for a certain prolongation of the note, and coincide with the *t* in MSS. where the Letters are used. Examples of these are given in the Table on the third *virga*, the second *clivis* and *porrectus*, the third and fourth *podatus*, and the second *torculus resupinus*, and are distinct from mere heads to the neums as in the last specimens of the *virga*, *scandicus*, and *climacus*.

No time-value at all is shown in the ordinary notation, the tails of certain notes being only the survival of the original *virga*, the head of which developed into the square note. Lozenges too *have quite the same time-value* as square notes, for they originated simply in peculiarities of handwriting, and in some MSS. the notes are in fact all lozenge shaped.

At first all the letters of the gamut were used as clefs, but now the clefs **C** **ｦ** and **b** placed at the beginning of the staff indicate that the notes on the line on which **C** is placed and on the line through the lower bar of **ｦ** are C and F, and that in the space where **b** stands is B♭. The notes above or below range accordingly in the diatonic scale without any interpolation of accidentals except an occasional B♭. When the ♭ is an accidental its force is never continued beyond the note or neum in which it occurs; when it is used as a clef, of course

TABLE OF NEUMS.

virga

punctum

clivis

porrectus

porrectus flexus

podatus

torculus

torculus resupinus

scandicus

climacus

pes
subpunctis

strophicus „ ,,, ///

epiphonus

quilisma

cephalicus

pressus

ancus

it continues throughout the melody. A guide ⌐ at the end of
the staff shows the note with which the next line of music
begins.

Double and single bars are modern inventions to mark
the close of phrases, or *distinctions*, of which they indicate
the relative importance and consequent *rallentando* of the
closing notes, and the length of the following pause. Half-
bars are used as breathmarks.

It is evident that, as the ordinary notation affords no guide
to the rendering of the chant beyond the grouping of the
notes, we must look to the neums for indications of the rhythm.
The only rules given by early writers are that *all notes are
short except the last which is long*, that there must be *no pause
between the syllables of a word*, and that *the pauses at the end
of distinctions must be well marked*. These are clearly only
the apophthegms of a good singing master, but they must be
strictly obeyed or the chant loses all its rhythm. Accent is
however an essential part of rhythm, so the neums must be
properly accented, and those of two or three notes are consequently of easy execution. The Metronome is about 184 for
the single notes, and the accent on the first note of a neum is
made *not by extra duration but by extra loudness*. The notes
are essentially all of equal time-value, but the neums, and the
Romanian Letters or Signs on them, indicate variations
of *tempo*, some of which are shown in the square notation.
The *epiphonus* ♪ and the *cephalicus* ♪ are forms of the
podatus ♪ and *clivis* ♪ which are used when the second
note is shortened by being merged in the pronunciation of
the word: *e.g.* a *podatus* on *Ho*-ly, as the *o* is a pure vowel,
would replace an *epiphonus* occurring on *Sanc*-tus, because
the consonants *nc* absorb the sound. The *ancus* ♪ is another
form of *liquescent* where the second and third notes are
shorter than in ♪♦♦. Sometimes a liquescent is used where
other versions of the melody give no indication of a second
note, as in the last note on *por* in the Gradual *Tollite portas*
(p. (27)). This probably indicates only a slight reduplication
of the note for the right pronunciation of the *r*.

The *quilisma* ∎ is always between two notes a minor third apart, and its effect is to *lengthen* these while it is sung *very lightly* itself. It was possibly a slight turn, or similar ornament, leading to the upper note, and is therefore frequently omitted in MSS. in the square notation.

The *strophicus* ∎∎ or ∎∎∎ is rendered by touching the penultimate note very lightly, probably a quarter-tone below the note as written. It always stands alone, and so will not be confounded with the *pressus* preceded by another neum *e.g.* by the *clivis* ⌐∎∎. The effect of the *pressus* is to shorten the previous neum, and, as its name implies, to acquire a very long and strong accent itself. In addition to the neums shown in the Table there is the *oriscus* ∎, of which the effect is to shorten and lower the preceding note so that ⌐∎∎ might almost be written ∎. Such are the deviations from equal time-value which are shown in the square notation, but the neums indicate others of which the laws have not yet been formulated. It appears however in most places that, where notes are lengthened by the Romanian Signs, it is in accordance with the rule for a *rallentando* before a pause, and in others the taste of a good singer leads to the same result. Plainsong is essentially *recitative*, and even for modern compositions in this species modern notation is quite inadequate.

The only other simple neum which calls for remark is the *scandicus*, which is written in two different ways of which the first and third forms given in the Table are best translated by ∎⌐ where the last note is held *very* slightly longer than when the form called the *salicus* ∎ is used.

The compound neums of more than three notes are less easy of analysis than those we have considered, though their practical rendering generally *solvitur ambulando*. The chief thing to remember is that a neum, like a word, has only one real accent, and unlike a word, *always* on its *first* note.

Therefore, although it is impossible to sing more than three notes rhythmically without putting in a second accent, any subsidiary accents must be of the lightest possible description. Continental authorities scarcely admit them to be accents, so afraid are they of too much weight being attached to them. In the same way however as *consubstantiálem* has minor accents on the first and third syllables as well as the full tonic accent on the fifth, so a long neum like the *pes subpunctis* 🎵 or 🎵 must have a secondary accent. Some of the English MSS. use a lozenge with a small tail upwards, ✔ but there seems to be no law in the matter, though it may be desirable to adopt this sign as a mark of the minor accent. The Romanian Signs however show plainly where the secondary accent should fall, and when fully studied will doubtless enable us to formulate some rules. In the meantime it appears as if the secondary accent in the *pes subpunctis* should be generally on the third note, as in *laudability*, except when the fourth note is the dominant of the mode and consequently attracts the accent, as in *omnipotential*. In the *porrectus flexus* and *torculus resupinus* the secondary accent is on the third note though in some cases the fourth note in the latter is also a little sustained. This effect of an *almost imperceptible* extra value being given to a note is often apparent when it is higher than the note on which the next syllable, and that unaccented, begins. It must however be as slight as possible, for a chief characteristic of good plainsong chanting is the rapid and easy passage from one word to another, and *a fortiori* from one syllable to another. It is therefore *only the first note* in a neum which, by being sung *louder* than the others, has an appreciable accent.

It will be seen that at present the good rendering of plainsong depends a great deal on the thorough acquaintance of the choirmaster with the music, and in fact he should study all examples of the melismatic chant with the aid of a MS. containing the Romanian Signs such as is being published at

Solesmes in *facsimile*.[1] But the simpler music is perfectly easy of execution if the few following rules be attended to :—

1°. Learn the melody so that it may be sung almost without book, and sing it quickly and *legato*. The single notes will then be given only the right time-value for the pronunciation of the syllables, and the neums on syllables will not be laboured

2°. Attend carefully to the breathing, and so make no pause in the middle of *distinctions*. The sentences will then flow easily "after the manner of distinct reading."

3°. Accent the first note of each neum by making it *louder* not *longer* than the others, and attend to the reflex action of the *quilisma, pressus*, and *oriscus*.

4°. Make *rallentandos* and good pauses at the end of *distinctions*, and sing the last notes *pianissimo* and *sostenuto*.

5°. Take care of the accented syllables and notes, and the others will take care of themselves.

The quickest *tempo* for melismatic plainsong is about Met. 184 to the single note, but it depends on the judgment of the Choirmaster, and melodies containing, as some do, many instances of the *strophicus* require a more dignified rendering. *Crescendo* and *diminuendo* may also be used *ad lib.* in melismatic chant, but the Psalter should be chanted as simply as possible. Lastly, if plainsong be properly sung, every syllable can be heard distinctly.

---

[1] Vol. IV. of *Paléographie Musicale.*

RHYTHM.

In the earliest days of Plainsong, Rhythm played as important a part as it does in modern measured music ; and it was only when men began to sing in parts that its beautiful and delicate accentuation and rhythm were lost. With the development of counterpoint, all idea of rhythm in the *cantus firmus* or Plainchant disappeared ; and hence we find Orni·thoparcus in 1516 laying down the rule that "All the notes of the Plainsong are to be sung in equal length and without accent or rhythm" and again Zarlino in 1579, saying " Plain-song must be sung without any variation of the time." [1] Under these conditions it served as the framework upon which were raised most of the works of that magnificent school of con-trapuntal Music which culminated in Palestrina, into which regular rhythm scarcely entered, and whose effects depended on the artistic intertwining of various melodies above and below the fixed notes of the *cantus firmus* or Plainchant.

But plainsong deprived of contrapuntal accessories, and sung in notes of equal length and without accent, becomes a meaningless and monotonous succession of sounds ; it is sung thus at the present day in St. Peter's at Rome, as in most churches on the Continent, and the beauty of the voices does little towards making it attractive.

The recent labours of the eminent Dom Pothier and other members of the Benedictine order have shown that in the earliest times Gregorian music was not sung in this way, and that it had a very distinct and beautiful rhythm of its own, differing from the ancient rhythm of Greek poetry and music in several important respects, but founded on the same principles of balance and proportion in the phrases and periods, and the use of the *Cæsura*.

---

[1] Zarlino *Opera* Venice 1579 vol. I. *p*. 24.

Rhythm means the regular flow of sound or language. This regularity is made appreciable by a more or less symmetrical division into certain small portions of the time occupied by a musical or poetical work of art. Hence the word rhythm is applied to the proportion, balance, and symmetry, between the various portions of the composition. The Romans also applied the word to rhetorical compositions, having regard to the balance and symmetry of the sentences and periods: and this is the sense in which we have to apply it to Gregorian music.

Rhythm may be divided into two classes: Strict, as used in poetry, measured music, and dancing; Free, as used in prose, or prose-poetry like the Psalms, and in most Gregorian music.

Strict rhythm demands an equal distribution of the time-values of the smaller portions of a musical composition, or of the accents of poetry.

Free rhythm demands a rough general balance of syllables, accents, and phrases in a prose composition, and of the divisions which correspond with these in plainsong.

On examining the general principles which underlie rhythm of every kind, it will be seen that Gregorian music obeyed the same fundamental principle of dividing time into more or less symmetrical portions by means of accents, cæsuras, and other details, as is found in the strict rhythm of modern music and poetry.

The smallest division of time which can be used for rhythm, consists of two portions, one of which is accented, the other unaccented. This division was anciently called the foot; its modern equivalent is the simple bar in music, which is either two-time, three-time, or four-time. But the modern bar may be compound, that is, it may contain more than one simple bar or foot; hence it is convenient for the present purpose to use the ancient term *foot* in preference to *bar* for the smallest rhythmical division of music. Whatever kind of foot, whether 2 time, 3 time, or 4 time, is used in any given composition, every foot in that piece, or in any principal portion of it, must be of equal time value, except where *rallentandos* or pauses occur, which, however, do not alter the character of the foot.

Several feet, usually four, are combined to form a definite section corresponding exactly with the Greek *colon* or rhythmical member : and several of these sections are again combined to form the *period*. The sections are clearly seen in poetry, in which the *cola* are written in separate lines, and called *verses* ; and the combination of several *verses* forms a *strophe*. (The word *verse* is used in its classical sense ; not in its modern sense of a group of several lines of poetry.)

Now, there is this distinction between the rhythm of measured music, and that of poetry : that while in measured music the feet must all be of exactly equal time-value amongst themselves, in modern poetry this need not be the case; for the rhythm of poetry depends on accent, and not on quantity, while that of modern music, like the poetry of the ancient Greeks, depends on both accent and quantity.

As long as we give the right number of accents to each verse, it does not matter what quantity, that is, what duration of time, we give to this or that foot or syllable, within reasonable limits. It can be shown historically that the modern form of poetry, in which quantity is neglected, and accent gives the rhythm, arose contemporaneously with plainsong upon the ruins of the old Greek Metrical poetry and music.

In all rhythm, whether strict or free, accent forms a most important ingredient, for without it rhythm could not exist. In the rhythm of music, the accents recur at regular intervals, and bars are drawn across the stave to show their position. But the group of notes within a single modern bar only exceptionally forms a rhythmical section of any kind. The single foot *can* begin and end within the compass of a single bar, as in the commencement of 'the slow movement of Schubert's quartet in D minor, which is almost entirely composed of dactyls ;—

But far more frequently the individual foot, like the whole phrase, commences somewhere within a bar, and finishes in another, as in the anapæstic rhythm of the last movement of Schumann's Piano quintet in E flat;—

where the bar-lines occur *within* the single feet, and not *between* them.   That portion of the phrase which comes before the first accent, has been called the *anacrusis*, a word which, as applied to music, means the first up beat (if any) of a single musical phrase.

Several feet, usually four, are combined to form a colon or rhythmical member : or, in other words, the ordinary colon consists of a succession of four accents, with their accompanying unaccented notes.   But a colon may also contain three, five, or six accents, although these forms are far rarer in modern music than that of four feet.

Two or more cola are again combined to form what is called a period ; and the combination of several periods forms a considerable portion of a composition corresponding with the strophe of poetry.

The application of these principles to prose and rhetoric, and to plainsong in its original form, may now be considered.

The ear and mind would become utterly bewildered if a whole page of prose were read, or recited, without any accents, and without a stop.   Hence the necessity for dividing it into

D

sentences and words, each sentence having its stop, and each word having its proper accentuation. In good prose, there is, besides a careful choice of words and ideas, a balance in the sentences, phrases, and paragraphs, just as in good music there is symmetry and balance in the cola and periods, and in the accentuation of the individual feet.

" It would be insufferable, even if it were possible, that an orator should make a whole speech in a single breath. A certain balance of phrases called *number*, has to be determined by the cultivated speaker, who divines it by a kind of instinct." [1] "This number is not that of verse, but it imitates that of verse." [2] " Good prose rhythm" says Aribo, "requires that there should be a rough balance in the number of syllables, and naturally also of accents in the members of sentences ; but they are not to be subjected to the rigorous laws of metre."

As the accentuation of plainsong, (and consequently its rhythm), depends so very largely upon the right accentuation of the words to which it is allied, the first thing necessary to know in order to analyse it, is the right accentuation of the Latin language : and in singing plainsong to English words, the same principles must be applied as far as possible. It must be remembered however that a group of English words will often be equal to one long Latin word, as in the case of *consubstantiálem*, which is translated by the four English words, " being of one substance."

Every word in Latin has one principal accented syllable, to which all other syllables are subordinate. [3] The only exceptions to this rule are as follows :

Conjunctions at the beginning of a sentence, or member of a sentence, are unaccented, even if they are of two syllables.

If however they are separated from the rest of the sentence by a stop, then they are accented.

If conjunctions are not at the beginning of a sentence, they are accented.

---

[1] Cicero, *De oratore.*
[2] Guido Aretino, *Micrologus.*
[3] Cicero, *De oratore.*

Relative pronouns, if they only express a simple relation, are unaccented.

But if they have no antecedent expressed, or if they are interrogative, then they are accented.

Prepositions, if they immediately precede the word which they govern, have no accent. If they are separated from it, or placed after it, they are accented.

In words of two syllables, the accent is placed on the first syllable as *páter, Déus, fídes, fínis*, etc.

In words of more than two syllables, the position of the accent depends on the metrical quantity of the penultimate syllable.

If the penultimate is long, it takes the accent, as *beátus, coróna, amícus*.

If it is short, the accent is on the antepenultimate, as *fácilis, vidébitur, miséricors, mulíeres*.

The accent never occurs earlier than the antepenultimate. Poets often take licences : but these cannot be allowed in prose.

Genitives in *íus* always take the accent on the *i*; as *ipsíus, illíus*, with the exception of *altérius*, which has the accent on the antepenultimate.

The three enclitics, *que, ne*, and *ve*, have a remarkable peculiarity. According to the ancient grammarians, these particles cause the accent to be placed on the final syllable of the word to which they are joined, even if that syllable be short, thus : *hominésque, meministíne, volucrésve*.

When several accented syllables follow one another, which of course can only happen when one or more of the words is a monosyllable, all the accents must be properly observed, as *Tú és Déus*, not *Tu es Déus*.

The monosyllables which are declinable, as *tu, me, vos*, etc. must each have an accent.

Further particulars on this subject may be found in the eighth chapter of Dom Pothier's book *Les Mélodies Grégoriennes*.

Thus far as to accent.   Is it necessary to observe quantity in plainsong?

The accentuation is what gives to each word its vitality. It is an element of nature, while quantity is an entirely conventional matter.   Now it often happens in plainsong, just as in modern music, that in the same word, while the long syllable is sung to a single note, the short syllable is sung to a considerable number of notes.   This at once disposes of any observance of verbal quantity.

It has been shown that the fundamental principle of strict rhythm is a numerical division into feet, cola, periods and strophes.   The free rhythm of prose and plainsong simply consists of a more free distribution of the corresponding portions.   The words, each of which contains one accent, correspond with the feet ; and where there are unimportant words such as prepositions, which do not receive an accent, they must be considered as syllables grouped round the accent of the word preceding or succeeding them.   These unaccented words may either come after the accented word, in which case they would be analogous to the dactyl or trochee of music ; or before it, when they would correspond with the anapæst or iambus.   The groups of words forming a portion of a sentence will correspond with the groups of feet forming a colon ; and the whole sentence will correspond with the musical period.   It will be useful to analyse a few examples of Syllabic Plainsong—that is, plainsong in which each syllable is sung to a single note, with only an occasional group of two or more notes.   This kind of plainsong depends entirely on the words for its rhythm and accentuation.   If the words are first read through with proper enunciation, and then sung to the plainsong melody, with exactly the same accentuation, and with a slight *rallentando* and *diminuendo* on the last two or three notes of each sentence, the proper rendering will be obtained : for Syllabic Plainsong is nothing more than a regulation of the natural rise and fall of the speaking voice by musical intervals.

In the Psalm verse *Lord remember David : and all his trouble,* it will be seen that, like nearly every other Psalm verse, it is in two portions, the first of which *Lórd remémber Dávid* contains three words and three accents, while the second contains four words, *and áll his tróuble,* with accents on *áll* and *tróuble:* for, following the Latin rule, the unimportant words may be considered as being unaccented. The balance here is three accents against two : and this kind of construction will be found in nearly every verse of the Psalms.

A high number of accents, such as nine, is rarely balanced against a low number, such as three ; and where this does occur, a return is immediately made in the succeeding verses to a more even proportion. In the Psalm-verse *Héar my vóice, O Gód in my práyer : presérve my lífe from féar of the énemy,* the balance is four accent-groups against four. The 15th verse of Psalm XVIII *The springs of the waters were seen, &c.* contains the unequal numbers of nine accents against four ; but at v. 16 a return is made to the even balance of four against four.

Again, in the Creed, following the same method of analysis, the groups of syllables round the accents in each phrase roughly balance one another in the same way, and it will be seen that the principle of irregular grouping of syllables round each accent is carried into the plainsong melody, which produces a still greater irregularity by the introduction of occasional short groups of notes on the same syllable(¹)·

We must now come to the analysis of what is called Melismatic Plainsong, in which groups of notes are sung to the single syllables, while only occasionally a syllable is sung to a single note. This kind of plainsong is far more difficult to sing than any other, but at the same time it is of much greater æsthetic and artistic value. Unfortunately space does not permit of going into all the details of melismatic plainsong, and a few general rules must suffice. The

(¹) See *Missa Rex splendens* (Masters).

accentuation here depends more on the music than the words.
As a rule, each separate group of notes should receive an
accent on its *first* note, and the other notes of the group must
flow easily from it, without any jerking or forcing of the voice.
The notation is intended to be a kind of pictorial representa-
tion of how each group is to be sung, showing how they are
bound together in a series of short phrases of varying lengths.
The shapes of the notes vary, but this variation *has nothing
to do with any differences in their time-value*. Notes of a
diamond shape always belong to the group or note which
immediately precedes them. When a *pressus* occurs, the
strong accent is attracted away from the first note of the
group preceding the pressus, and given to the pressus which,
as its name implies, is slightly dwelt upon.

The music is divided into short phrases by means of
bar lines, which however must be carefully distinguished
from modern bar lines, with which they have nothing in
common. These phrases are called *distinctions*. If the bar
line extends over only a portion of the stave, the distinction
is *minor*, and corresponds with the colon of measured music,
while if the bar extends over the whole of the stave the
distinction is *major*; a combination of two or more minor
into one major distinction corresponds with the *period* of
music. The half-bars showing minor distinctions are practically breathing marks. Double bars show where a principal portion ends, or where the chorus enters, or where
there is to be a repetition. Each minor distinction must
be sung in one breath if possible, and there must be a
slight rallentando and diminuendo on its last two or three
notes. A complete break in the sound must be made
between the distinctions, and nowhere else. But if a distinction is too long to be sung in one breath, a half breath
may be taken between any two of its neums, not within them.
On no account must breath be taken just before a new syllable
in the course of a word; it must be taken at the beginning
of the minor distinction which contains the syllable in ques-

tion. This precept was called by the ancients the "Golden Rule." No one of the intermediate notes of a neum is to be dwelt upon either by extension of its time-value or by accentuation, except in the case of the *strophicus* and *pressus*, in which the sound should be extended in accordance with the number of notes on the same degree of the scale. But there are certain cases in which a slight impulse, hardly amounting to an accent, may be made on one of the intermediate notes of a long descending group, as described on page 28.

We will now analyse the music of the Gradual *Tollite portas* (p. (27)) which is a good specimen of melismatic Chant. Placing an accent on the first note of each neum, the first distinction, consisting of the words *Tollite portas*, contains four principal accents, viz. one on the syllable *Tol*, and three on the syllable *por*. The next distinction *principes vestras* has two accents on *prin*, one on *ci*, one on *pes*, two on *ves*, one on *tras* : hence there is a balance of four accents against seven in the first two distinctions. But the syllable *tras* contains a long jubilation ; and as it would be impossible to sing from bar to bar here without taking breath, we shall have to separate the jubilation from the body of the phrase, by taking breath after the first clivis of *tras* : and the jubilation becomes a minor distinction, containing five accents.

The principal accents in the next distinction fall one each on *et* (owing to the strophicus) and *le*, two on *va*, three on *por*, and one on *ta*, eight in all : and this is answered by six in the succeeding distinction, distributed thus : one on *æ*, one on *na*, four on *les*.

After this we have one on *et*, four on *i* and, as we shall be again obliged to separate the jubilation from the rest of the distinction, it will be best to consider that the syllable *bit* has two accents, and ends with the second clivis : the jubilation contains only two principal accents in this case. This distinction then is divided into two portions of respectively six and two accent groups.

Then follows a distinction with a long jubilation, which may be considered to begin after the *pes subbipunctis* of the syllable *æ*; and the division is three accent groups on *Rex*, one on *glo*, one on *ri* and two on *æ*;—seven in all, against seven in the jubilation.

If we for the moment imagine the whole passage to be comparable to a stanza of poetry containing nine verses, or a passage of instrumental music containing nine phrases of irregular lengths, we get the following analysis of the accent-groups :

1. Tollite portas   ...   4 accent groups
2. Principes vestras ...   7   „   „
3. Jubilation   5   „   „
4. et elevamini portæ   8   „   „
5. æternales   6   „   „
6. et introibit...   ...   7   „   „
7. Jubilation   2   „   „
8. Rex gloriæ   ...   7   „   „
9. Jubilation   7   „   „ .

It is perhaps a little difficult for those accustomed to the more or less mathematically exact divisions of most modern poetry and modern music, to realise that in the above seeming disorder, there is an underlying principle of order and balance of the very highest artistic importance. It might be worth the student's while to compare it with some Greek choruses, in which, while the single feet are equal, the lengths of the verses often vary as much as the numbers of the accent-groups in Gregorian Melismatic Chant. The Greeks are generally acknowledged to have brought the theory and practice of rhythm to a higher degree of perfection than any of their successors; and as we know that the early Christians derived their musical scale from that of the Greeks, it would seem not impossible that the composers of the beautiful form of art known as plainsong were not entirely uninfluenced by the Greek feeling for variety in rhythm also.

We give as an example, a strophe from Euripides' "Alcestis," vv. 435 to 443, with Dindorf's metrical scheme translated into musical notation. (See G. Dindorfius, *Metræ*, *Æschyli Sophoclis Euripidi, etc.*, Oxon. 1842.)

1. ὦ   Πε-λί - ου   θύ-γα - τερ,

2. χαί - ρου - σά μοι   εἰν   'Α - ἴ - δα   δό - μοι - σι

3. τὸν ἀν - ά - λι-ον   οἶ - κον   οἰ - κε - τεύ - οις

4. ἴσ - τω δ''Α-ἴ-δας ὁ με - λα-γχαί-ρας θεὸς, ὃς ἐπὶ ἐώ-τᾳ

5. πη - δα-λί - ῳ   τε γί - ρων

6. νεκ - ρο - πομ - πὸς ἵ - ζει

7. πο - λὺ δὴ   το - λὺ δὴ   γυ - ναῖκ'   ἀ - ρίσ - ταν

8. λίμ - ναν 'Αχερ - ον - τί - αν πο-ρεύ - σας ἰλ-α - τᾳ δικ - ώ-τῳ

The rhythm here is what is called by Aristoxenus *dactylic* or *fourtime*; that is to say, there is the value of four short notes in each foot, or, as we should say, in each bar. Hence, if we take the quaver as representing the value of the short syllable or note, the time signature will be that of four quavers, or two crotchets in a bar, *i.e.* $\frac{2}{4}$. Thus far the metrical scheme is similar to that of a modern piece in $\frac{2}{4}$ time in which no note of less value than a quaver appears. But here the resemblance ceases. Instead of symmetrical phrases of four bars each, as in most modern compositions, we get phrases of unequal lengths, producing a variety of rhythmical schemes in the various verses, such as is rarely found in modern music, but is found in plainsong, and is an element of great beauty to

those who can accustom themselves to it. The scheme of
musical accents in the above strophe is as follows :

Verse 1 contains 3 accents.

,,	2	,,	4	,,
,,	3	,,	4	,,
,,	4	.,	6	,,
.,	5	,,	3	,,
,,	6	,,	3	,,
,,	7	,,	4	,,
,,	8	,,	7	,,

In several of the longer verses Dindorf places a comma, to
show the position of the *Cæsura*, or place for breaking the
verse in order to take breath. The portions marked by the
cæsura practically answer to the *minor distinctions* of the
Gregorian Chant, while the whole verse answers to the *major
distinction*. It will thus be seen that while the ancient Greek
rhythm as a rule corresponded with modern musical rhythm
as to the single feet, in the variety of its verses or phrases it
corresponded more with plainsong ; while plainsong in its
turn, breaking away from the mathematical division of equal
feet or bars, made use of the same variety in the single accent
groups (which roughly correspond with feet or bars) as is
found in the prose utterances of a good orator. The absence
of Harmony from both Greek and early Christian music
rendered it absolutely necessary for musicians to make use of
rhythm as one of their chief means of producing variety. We
are most of us familiar with the monotony that is produced
by a constant reiteration of four bar phrases, if no variety of
harmonic effects is used in them ; and this monotony would
be increased tenfold if there were no harmony at all. Hence
it is found that in all music in which harmony has not been
developed, great stress is laid on rhythm ; and in many cases,
as in Indian music for example, very complicated rhythms
occur, which would be beyond the comprehension of any
modern European audience.

STRUCTURE.

To obtain a right understanding of the structure of plainsong we must examine the simpler forms of the chant, and trace from them the development of the more elaborate melodies. The simplest complete form is the Psalm Tone; but before considering what the Tones *are* it may be advisable to see what they are *not* by examining an Anglican Chant.

Christ Church Tune.

It will be seen that it consists of the reciting note and two bars of fixed rhythm for the mediation, then another reciting note, which need not be the same as in the first half, followed by three bars in fixed rhythm. The notes at first may have retained their original free character, for in 1664 the time-signature was not prefixed, nor was the chant barred up, but afterwards they gained a strict time-value, and the reciting note was given a fixed rhythmical value of two bars. The first half of an Anglican Chant accordingly contains four bars of two-time measure, and the second half five bars. It is only this proportion in the accents of four to five which renders at all endurable the repetition of the same short melody through a long psalm. If the Anglican Chant were in the ordinary four-feet measure of modern music it would soon fall out of use. Its plainsong characteristics alone preserve it from the attacks of Gregorianists, who, however, considerably weaken their case by a general want of appreciation of the strong points of the Tones, which are consequently converted into merely bad Anglican Chants.

The structure of a Tone is, however, essentially different from that of a Chant, inasmuch as it is based on the mono-toning of a Psalm verse, and has consequently no feeling of time-value or fixed rhythm. The pointing in the MSS. appears to be governed by the following rules:—

1° There was a *rallentando* on the penultimate note or notegroup of the ending, and it consequently received the accented syllable nearest to the final.

2° The preceding notes or notegroups were allotted singly to the preceding syllables, so that the accents on them varied as the accents of the syllables, as in the endings of Tones 1 and 4 (pp. (7) & (9)). ·

3° But, as the elevation of the voice implies an accent, if the note after the reciting note ascended, the syllabic rule yielded to its attraction of an accented syllable with a con-sequent filling in of those that are not accented.

4° The simple endings, consisting of one note to a syllable, were elaborated by the conversion of the single notes into note-groups, which, save exceptionally, were never split up among separate syllables. On the other hand the separate notes of inflections could not be combined into groups on a syllable.

The mediations were treated on the same principles as the endings, except that as the *rallentando* at their close was less important, rule 1° did not apply.

The 4th ending of the 4th Tone is an extreme example of the variability of accent, for as it contains three notes before the penultimate, the accent may either fall on the first after the reciting note, as in *imágine a vain thing*, or on the second, as *Lord with hóly worship*, and sometimes even on the third, as *of all thy márvellous works*, so that two accents as it were come together, or unaccented syllables fall on the penultimate note. This difficulty is common both to Latin and English, and the explanation of its solution is that the strene on the penultimate note, according to rule 1°, is not an accent but a *rallentando*.

Returning to the *Christchurch Tune* it will be seen that it consists really of harmonies to the First Tone 4th ending, which is in the Tenor part. The first note of the bar after the reciting note is the last note of the real reciting note, and the second note is in fact the first of the mediation. Now this note, when the Tone is properly chanted, may be accented or not as circumstances require, but the tyranny of the Anglican Chant demands that it shall never be accented at all. Again in the ending the first note after the reciting note should rightly vary in its accentuation, but the Anglican Chant insists that it shall always be accented. All variety is thereby lost, and when the Tones came to be sung in this way they ceased to be recitation with inflections, and were only very dreary tunes.

The Psalters until now in use are pointed according to the taste of the Editors, and follow no rules, if we except one which has copied the method invented by the editors of the Mechlin Service Books, which is almost that of an Anglican Chant. But there is no difficulty in tracing in 13th century MSS. the exact system that was then followed, and all difficulties that exist in the English words may be found in the Latin. The MSS. recognise and solve them, and we cannot do better than follow their teaching. At the time they were written Christians had chanted the psalms daily for centuries, and we may be sure that their ears were better attuned to delicacies of chanting than ours can possibly be. It is indeed surprising to find how extremely acute their perceptions were, and in difficult cases where two methods of pointing were open for choice, one is invariably forced to confess that the MSS. are justified in their selection.

In chanting the Psalms we must above all remember that we are dealing with prose and not with poetry. We have not therefore to *sing* them as we sing a metrical litany, for which an Anglican Chant is eminently suited, but to *read* them.

The voices naturally blend together on one note for the greater part of the verse, and by an easy development a slight change is made from it at the mediation and ending. At these inflections however the voice must not break off from reading into singing. The whole verse must continue in the same style without any increase or lessening of the speed at which the separate syllables are chanted. This effect will be obtained if care is taken not to make the slightest pause before beginning the inflections, but to pass on immediately from the last reciting note to the first note of the inflection, whether it be accented or not.([1]) A good pause at the colon gives dignity to the chanting (an old rule was that it should be long enough to say *Ave Maria*), and if the last notes of the mediation and ending be properly sustained and sung *pianissimo*, they produce the right effect of restfulness which is very important. The verses may be sung antiphonally between both sides of the Choir, or between one or more cantors and the full choir with the people. Chiefly we must remember that the Tones are not intended to be pretty melodies like Anglican Chants. They are simply changes in the pitch of the voice in which we *read*—not *sing*—the Psalms.

The Introit forms of the Tones show a further development by using an intonation to both parts of the verse and by amplifying the notes of the inflections; but the form of Psalmody used for the Tracts is the most elaborate, while it still retains most plainly the characteristics of (*a*) intonation, (*b*) recitation, and (*c*) inflection. In the Example given on page (25) the intonation falls on the opening syllables with particular attention to the first possible accent, and the inflection is given to the last three syllables of the text. Intermediate words are allotted to the reciting note, which is expanded into four notes on the first syllable after the intonation, and afterwards into two notes on accented syllables. It is more difficult to trace these characteristics in more elaborate examples of plainsong, but they nevertheless exist as shown below with regard to the Gradual *Tollite*.

---

(1) A good rule for choirmen accustomed to the ordinary bad style of chanting is "sing the reciting note slowly and the inflections quickly." This will give evenness of recitation.

But we will first examine an elaboration of the simpler Tone-form in the Ordinary of the Mass.([1])

The Creed is of the simplest character, and consists of the intonation and a reciting note with a certain number of inflections. These musical phrases are repeated several times, and where the text requires, are shortened by omitting some notes, or where necessary, lengthened by addition or repetition. A parallel to this is found in the mediations of the 3rd and 7th Tones where a note is omitted if necessary, or extra syllables are filled in on the reciting note to which the mediations return. *The Father Almighty, And invisible, The only begotten Son of God,* are all founded on the same melodic phrase, but in the last there are additional notes on *begotten.* This, in its Ambrosian and Gregorian forms, was the only chant to the Creed in use until the 14th century, and it is extremely simple so that the people should have no difficulty in singing it. The chants to the *Gloria in Excelsis* are more numerous and elaborate, but have still the same characteristics. The melodies to the *Sanctus* and *Agnus* are still more florid, but not so much so as those to the *Kyries.* A good and elaborate example of the latter is the Kyrie *Rex Splendens* composed by S. Dunstan, or, as the legend says, heard by him as sung by the Angelic Choir. The first *Kyrie* is the simplest, the *Christe* is a repetition of it with some additions at the beginning, and the next *Kyrie* has still further notes added in the introduction, thus expressing a gradual exaltation of feeling as the *Kyries* proceed, which is extremely effective. The 11th century Troper at Corpus Christi College, Cambridge, contains harmonies in neums to the 2nd and 8th *Kyries* (p. (25)) and 2nd *Christe.* These harmonies are in contrary motion to the melody, and are the earliest known of this species of counterpoint. It is unfortunate that they are not also in the alphabetic notation, for as they stand at present, any restoration must be in great part conjectural.

It was the custom in the tenth century to add words or *farses* to the *Kyries*; a syllable was fitted to a note, *e.g.*, to this

[1] See *Missa Rex Splendens* Plainsong edition (Masters).

melody *Kyrie rex splendens celi arce salve jugiter et clemens plebi tue semper eleyson.* The accentuation of the various farses set to the same melody differs so greatly that it seems probable the Latin accents were adapted to those of the music, which of course were well known; and it is possible to do this in most cases without extreme violence to the text. Our English *Kyrie* has one unvarying farse, and we can therefore in adapting, so group the notes that the accents of the original unfarsed melody are preserved. Artistically it would be preferable to adapt the music to the simple *Lord have mercy*, but it is at least probable that our invariable farse goes as smoothly to the original melody as did the syllabic farses of the Middle Ages.

We will now turn to the more ornate and variable portions of the Mass. It is often supposed that the Ambrosian Chant is all of the simple character of the Ambrosian Tones and Hymns. But this is incorrect, for the melodies in Ambrosian MSS. (*see* Brit. Mus. Add 34,209) show that even in the fourth century the Church used music as florid as any in the Gregorian Antiphonale, which no doubt incorporated many Ambrosian melodies. Of these a good example is the Office (or Introit) of the Mass for the Dead. According to the theorists it should be in the 6th mode, but as it never descends below the final—F—which is also the final of the 5th mode, there is no reason for this ascription except that the prevailing note is A, which is the dominant of the 6th mode. The insertion of the B♭ puts it into the ordinary major scale which is really the old Greek Second or Lydian mode.

Another instance of the transfer of an Ambrosian melody to the Gregorian Antiphonale is that which is used for the Gradual *Justus ut palma* and several others (p. (27)). In the Ambrosian Chant it is set to *A summo cœlo* on the 2nd Sunday in Advent, and to the same words as a Gregorian Gradual. It is attributed to the second mode transposed a fifth higher, and the final and dominant are therefore A and C—the transpositions of D and F—and the range of the mode E to e. The intonations vary, but suggest the tetrachords of the allied 1st and 2nd modes, and the mode is at once fixed

by the rise to the dominant C on the first syllable of *portas* (in
the Gradual *Tollite*) which is sung to three triplets closing in the
neumatic notation on a liquescent B, which in this case is probably only a slight reduplication of the same note for the proper
pronunciation of the *r*, and is therefore often not noted in the
square notation. This is one of the instances of the extreme
delicacy of the earliest notation, showing its exactness in bringing out the right enunciation of the syllables. In *A summo cœlo*
there is no liquescent neum here as *cœ* is a pure vowel sound.
The last syllable closes on the final. *Principes* again rises to the
dominant and closes on the sub-final G. Note that although
the first syllable contains the same number of notes as the
last, it has two strong accents, while the last consists of a
compound neum, and has consequently only one, the B♭
which careless singers might accent, being marked with the
Romanian Letter signify *celeriter*. *Vestras* takes up the
melody on the same note, and, circling round the final,
begins the *jubilation* on the third note of *tras*, making a
cadenza on the dominant, where it at last rests on the pressus
before the torculus on the final A. The first C in this *jubilation* is possibly either a *quarter-tone* below, or it may be an
anticipation, or it may be *tied* to the following note. There
are no sufficient data at present to determine, but the effect of
any one of the three renderings is about the same to our
modern ear. The quilisma on the B is also an unknown term,
though the shape of the neum would seem to imply that it
contained three grace notes (B A B). It is translated as a
quaver, but it should be sung as of rather less value, and the
notes before and after it will consequently gain in prominence.
It is noteworthy that the *jubilations* at the end of distinctions were phrases well-known to the singers, being often
repeated to different melodies in the same mode, and are
therefore frequently omitted in the neumatic MSS. At the
close of the distinction a good pause must be made, and the
concluding notes sung *rallentando* and *pianissimo*. The next
distinction begins with a strophicus, which again may be
rendered in three different ways, and a similar repeated note
occurs on *va*, but here the MSS. of the School of Metz
translate the first C as a B. This difference in traditions

E

favours the theory of the note being the quarter tone below C.
There is a stroke over either clivis on *va*, so that the first note
of each is long, as shown in the translation by >. The same
symbol is used to indicate the lengthening of A, the note
which precedes the quilisma in *portæ*, and the stroke over the
clivis D A is translated by a crotchet.

The three notes on *æ* of *æternales* are the translation
of the three dots of the *trigon*, which seems to be a
torculus of which the first note is a quarter-tone below the
second. This is another doubtful neum but its rendering does
not make much difference in the chant. On the *na* we get a
full strophicus, and here it is almost certain that the middle
note is a quarter-tone lower than the others. It is made by a
triple movement of the throat, and if found too difficult for
choirs the note may be simply sustained for three beats. The
last syllable *les* begins with a long clivis of which the second
note is also lengthened and accented as it precedes a quilisma.
The next peculiarity is the oriscus on C which lowers and
shortens the preceding note, and attracts an accent, and
then follows a pressus on D before the distinction closes on
the dominant C. It will be noticed that the cadences in
plainsong generally descend, as the tonality has no feeling of
the *leading note* of the modern major scale. In the next
distinction it may be noted that in the second neum on *i*
formed of a podatus and climacus combined, the podatus is an
anacrusis with a weak accent leading up to the strong accent
on the E. The first C in *bit* is specially marked *celeriter* as
there would be a tendency to accent it. The remaining
portion of the Gradual given in the example presents no other
special features of interest, except that it may be noted that it
once overpasses the range of the mode by rising to F, and
that in English MSS. a C takes the place of the quilisma in
the final torculus, thus showing the indeterminate character of
the neum.

In the translation the student must supply an imaginary
slur over every note-group, so that their first notes will be
well accented. But it cannot be too often repeated that no
modern notation can exactly express the rendering of plainsong, which depends in its minutiæ entirely on the feeling of

the singers, who by their acquaintance with the tonality know instinctively the notes that should have extra prominence.

As shown on page 40 the melody contains six major distinctions in which are included three jubilations, making nine accent-groups. Each distinction contains (*a*) an intonation, (*b*) a phrase of recitation, (*c*) an inflection, and (*d*) a closing note or note-group, which, except in the first and third distinctions, is expanded into a jubilation. The intonation introduces the melodic phrase, the recitation is sung to the following syllables, and the inflection begins on the *accented syllable* of the last word of the phrase allotted to the distinction. It will be noticed in the three examples given how the melody is fitted to the text either by compression or expansion, and how liquescents are introduced and omitted according to the exigencies of the syllables.

In conclusion a few words should be said about the plainsong melodies to the hymns, which stand on a different basis from true plainsong. The words are in the comparatively fixed rhythm of poetry, and the melodies should therefore be adjusted to the fixed accents, but with the same freedom of *tempo* which is granted to all singers of ballads, and which can only be obtained in choirs by singing in unison. This adaptation of the notes (however numerous on a syllable) to the poetical accents will thus produce an effect altogether different from that of modern hymns, which, for the right singing of the harmonies, must be sung with a mathematical precision of time-value to the syllables. Any time-value that may be found in plainsong hymns is, however, only in the period between the recurrence of the strong accents, the intermediate notes being quite *ad lib.* In an ordinary Long Measure stanza there are for instance two strong accents in each line—

> *O Blést Creator óf the light,*
> *Who mák'st the day with rádiance bright.*

Attention to these will give a rhythm to the poetry quite different from the four accents of a modern harmonised melody. No translation into modern notation of plainsong melodies to either prose or poetry can be really correct, but the following rules will suggest how the hymns may be rendered. Where two or three notes occur to a syllable there is no difficulty in giving the note-group the rhythmical value of the single syllable in the poetical metre, a strong accent being placed on the first note of the group. The same applies to longer groups of uniform motion, but when a neum of more than three notes first ascends and then descends the scale, the rendering is more doubtful and must be decided in each case on its merits and from internal evidence. In the third line of p. (18) No. 5 where the pressus occurs, the reduplication or sus-pension of the second note gives the effect of the Scotch Snap

 In more extended neums varieties in versions often seem to show that the ascending notes

were *appoggiaturas*, so that the first and second lines of *Eterne rex altissime* would almost be as follows :—

It must however be remembered that this version is only approximate, for the singing of a hymn in unison should be as much *ad libitum* as that of a ballad. In the above, for instance, the rendering of the latter half of the phrase a-b must of necessity be more deliberate than that of the corresponding one c-d, though in ordinary cases where the melodies more nearly correspond, as in the third and fourth lines, there is no appreciable difference in the duration of the intervals between the strong accents. It should also be remembered that even the component notes of the phrase have no mathematical time-value amongst themselves, so that in the second line the minim D is rather shorter, and the following crotchets C B rather longer, than as written. These rules will apply to the hymns proper, but the music of the sequences partakes partly of the character of the plainsong of prose and partly of that of hymns. The later sequences were simply hymns, and sometimes in triple time. The earlier ones of the ninth and tenth centuries, were however words set to a pre-existing plainsong melody, viz., that of an extra jubilation to the *Alleluia* of the Gradual, and as their rhythm is the free rhythm of the melismatic plainsong they are properly called *proses*. Of this latter class *Salus Eterna* (p. (21)) is a good example, and *Laudes Deo* (p. (22)) is a representative of the transition style. *Letabundus* and *Missus Gabriel* (p. (23)) are practically carols and should be so rendered. In all hymns and sequences we should remember that the notation is defective, for the composers had not yet invented a system of notation that would express time-value. The interpretation must therefore be in accordance with the words and the internal evidence of the music, and, as they were melodies that, when written, caught the ear of the people, if they fail to do so now the fault must be solely in our rendering of them.[1]

(1) The following ancient Dalecarlian melody kindly communicated by Professor Byström of Stockholm has a remarkable affinity to the elaborate hymns.

Så högt har Gud oss till stor fröjd Den fall - na
Att han sin son från him - lens höjd Har sändt, som
verl - den äl - skat. } I syn - der var så verl-den
oss har fräl - sat. }
sänkt Att hjelp ej stod att fin - na Ej nåd att vin -
- na, Om Gud sin son ej skänkt. O men-skal det be - sin - na.

PSALMODY.

Psalmody may be defined, for our present purpose, as the musical recitation of the Psalter. We propose, however, before going into the practical part of the subject, to say a few words on the different methods of performance which the Church employed in early times in her public worship.

The Psalms formed so prominent a constituent in the ancient Choir Services that, as has been happily said, " they might be considered as the *thread* upon which the *pearls* of lesson and collect were strung." S. Chrysostom's words, which Dr. Neale so aptly quotes at the opening of his Commentary on the Psalms, are doubtless familiar to many of us. " If we keep vigil in the Church, David comes first, last and midst. If early in the morning we seek for the melody of hymns, first, last and midst is David again. If we are occupied with the funeral solemnities of the departed, still David is first, last and midst." And he proceeds to show in how great estimation the Psalter was then held, and how it permeated not only the religious worship but the whole life of the Christians of that period, and was the chief stimulus with both young and old to the praise of Almighty God.

In these days we seem to have sadly degenerated. We hear a great deal about "bright and hearty services," but what is it that is supposed to constitute a bright and hearty service ? Not the inspired words of the Psalmist. It is no longer David that is 'first, last and midst.' His place has been usurped by the modern metrical Hymn, which is literally first, last and midst in many of our Churches, but which, whatever its merits, cannot claim to be inspired, any more than the hymn-*tune* of the " bright and hearty " order can be said to have any affinity with what an old writer calls the *Modulamen placidum* of the early Christian Psalmody.

There appear to have been four different methods of chanting the Psalms during the first four centuries.

The first method was when the whole psalm was sung by a single voice while the other worshippers sat and listened in silence. Cassian speaks of this as being the mode in which the Egyptian monks conducted their Psalmody, each one taking it in turn to sing one or more Psalms. This was called the *Cantus Tractus*, *i.e.* a sustained uninterrupted chant. A relic of this method of singing still exists, in name at least, in the Western liturgies of the Gregorian family (using the word Gregorian to distinguish them from the Ambrosian and Mozarabic liturgies). It is still called the *Tract*, though the original way of singing it *solo-wise* has long been abandoned.

Secondly, there was the *Direct* method or *Cantus Directaneus*. This was when the Psalm was sung straight through by the whole Choir (*Full*, as we should say). Instances of this are still to be found both in the Ambrosian and Benedictine Offices.

Thirdly, there was the *Responsorial* method. In this, (just as in the first method) the Psalm was chanted by one voice, in the earlier days generally by a deacon, later, by one in minor orders, either a sub-deacon or a *lector*. After every verse the people *responded* with an unvarying refrain, taken generally from the Psalm itself. Very often it was the first verse which formed this refrain, and this is probably the explanation of the word ἀκροστίχιον which is used in this connexion in the 'Apostolic Constitutions,' and which means the first words, or the top line. Some interesting allusions to this kind of chanting occur in the writings of many of the early Fathers, *e.g.* SS. Chrysostom, Basil, Athanasius, Ambrose and Augustin. It seems to have been a very common mode of rendering the Psalmody up to the close of the 4th century. Indeed it is said to have been the *only* method employed in the Western Church until the time of S. Ambrose. Like the two modes of chanting previously mentioned it has left its traces in the Service Books, both of

East and West. In the Breviaries of the Gregorian type especially it exists in the form of the Invitatory Psalm at Mattins. Whether the Responds which occur after the Lessons at Mattins in the Breviary, or that particular Respond which was sung from the steps of the Ambon after the Epistle at Mass, (and which was consequently called the 'Gradual') are the remains of the old *Psalmus Responsorius*, as some liturgiologists think, or whether they were of later growth, and purely Roman in their origin, as S. Isidore seems to imply, and as M. Batiffol maintains, we cannot determine. The elaborate character of their music would rather lead one to take the latter view.

The fourth, and by far the most important of the ancient methods of chanting the Psalms, was that which we call *Antiphonal.* Before touching on its history we may remark that there have been doubts raised of late as to whether the Antiphonal singing introduced by S. Ambrose at Milan in the latter part of the 4th Century was *really* the chanting of alternate choirs. There is a passage in Aristotle's *Problemata,* where the word *Antiphon* is defined as the "accord of an octave," and as we know on the testimony of S. Augustin that S. Ambrose derived his new method of chanting from the *Greeks*, it is suggested that the combined singing of men and women, singing each in their own register, *i.e.* in octaves, was what he introduced. It is doubtless true, that whereas in earlier times the women were strictly forbidden to take any part in the singing, S. Ambrose does make special mention of the hearty singing of 'men, women, maidens and children,' and compares it to the 'thunderous roar of the waves.' Tradition however is certainly against the theory that Antiphonal singing meant singing in octaves, and we may well be content with the generally-received definition given by S. Isidore as "*vox reciproca, id est duobus scilicet choris alternatim psallentibus,*" until some clearer proof to the contrary is forthcoming.

As to the history of this method of singing, (*i.e.* from the time of the Christian era, for no doubt it formed part of the

old Jewish ritual), Philo mentions that it was in use amongst
the "Therapeutæ," a body of Christian Ascetics at Alexandria
in the time of the Evangelist S. Mark, who was the first
Bishop there. In the next century we have the well-known
letter of the younger Pliny to the Emperor Trajan, reporting
that "the Christians in Bithynia were in the habit of assem-
bling before sunrise and chanting a hymn to Christ as God
by turns amongst themselves." It seems therefore not at all
improbable that Antiphonal chanting was in use in the time
of the Apostles themselves, who in their turn no doubt derived
it from the old Temple worship.

But now comes the question: Did Antiphonal chanting
originally consist in the mere alternate singing of the Psalms
themselves by two Choirs, verse and verse about, or rather
was it not *in substance* similar to the Responsorial method?
i.e. was it not the intercalation between each verse or two
of an unvarying refrain, taken from the Psalm itself, one side of
the Choir singing the verse of the Psalm, the other answering
with this refrain or Antiphon? This view appears the most
probable, and it accords best with the well known tradition of
the vision of S. Ignatius of Antioch, and with S. Basil's
description of the Psalmody at Cesarea. "Psallere cum
antiphona" or "cum antiphonis" is a common expression of
the early writers. Silvia, in the record of her liturgical
pilgrimage in 385-8, speaks of psalms *and* antiphons being
sung at the Church of the Resurrection at Jerusalem. Cassian
tells us of the custom in the 4th century of *lengthening out* the
Psalms with Antiphons. S. Chrysostom employed this method
of chanting, by way of opposing the heretical practice of
the Arians, who sang *their* Psalmody antiphonally, inter-
calating the verses with the blasphemous refrain, "And now
where are they that affirm that the Three are One?"
S. Chrysostom, I say, in opposition to this custom, authorized
the formulation of the Catholic belief in the Consubstantial
in the one word ὁμοούσιὸν, which he caused to be introduced
between the verses of the Psalms in his Cathedral Church of

S. Sophia at Constantinople.   And so we may fairly conclude
that it was this same Antiphonal method which was introduced by S. Ambrose at Milan in or about the year 380.

So much for the ancient *methods* of chanting.   Now as to
the music itself.   With the first three methods of which I
have spoken it is probable that the melodies were as a rule
very simple.   At any rate, we know that this was the case at
Alexandria, where S. Athanasius "caused the *lector* to
chant the Psalms with such slight inflections of the voice
that the effect was more like *distinct reading* than *singing*."
But S. Ambrose, along with the Antiphonal method, which
he borrowed from the Greeks, also, it is said, introduced the
Greek music, the sweetness of which, S. Augustin tells us, often
brought the tears to his eyes, though (he adds) he could not
help thinking sometimes that the severer style of singing
which prevailed in the time of Athanasius was safer, being
less likely to attract the attention of the hearers away from
the words.

We may now examine some specimens of Ambrosian
Psalm-tones.   (See p. (10) of examples.)   The Ambrosian
system recognized only four modes, and it is generally
said that these are identical with the four authentic modes
of the Gregorian system (*i.e.*, the 1st, 3rd, 5th and 7th), and
that S. Gregory added the plagal modes two centuries later.
But this seems to be a mistake.   There are many instances
of Ambrosian Melodies which might be said to be quite
as much in a plagal as in an authentic mode.   It would be
nearer the truth to say that a great portion of the Ambrosian
music lies within (or at least only occasionally oversteps) the
compass of the pentachord which is common to each authentic
mode and its corresponding plagal, in the Gregorian system.

The examples of the Ambrosian Psalm-tones given on
page (10) are not exhaustive, but they will suffice to illustrate
some of their principal characteristics.   (1) Unlike the
Gregorian Tones, they have neither intonation nor mediation.
In other words, the first half of the verse was always sung in

monotone, the second half only receiving a melodic cadence.
The monotonic mediation is represented by the double note ;
the letters under the endings are the vowels of *seculorum*,
Amen. (2) In each mode two or three dominants will be
found, *e.g.* in the 1st (which answers to the 1st and 2nd
Gregorian), *la, sol* and *fa* occur as dominants ; in the 2nd (*i.e.*
the Gregorian 3rd and 4th) two, *si* and *la* ; in the 3rd
(Gregorian 5th and 6th) three, *do, si* and *sol*; and in the 4th
(Gregorian 7th and 8th) two, *re* and *do*. (3) More curious
still, some of these tone-forms will be found in the MSS.
transposed a fifth lower, the Antiphon remaining in its normal
seat, the result being that the dominant and the final are the
same. (4) It will be noticed how the same cadence is used in
more than one mode. The last four notes *e.g.* of I. 2, II. 2,
IV. 1 and 3, are absolutely the same as regards their intervals.
In the same way the cadence of I. 6 and III. 1 are identical,
and also those of II. 1 and III. 3, from which it is evident
that but little variety was considered necessary, the Psalm-
tone being regarded merely in the light of a simple recitative,
having no *raison d'être* apart from its Antiphon.

From Milan the Antiphonal method quickly spread
throughout France and Spain, the Church in Rome itself,
always conservative and tenacious of old traditions, being the
last to give up the old Responsorial method and adopt the
new one. This, as we may infer from the *Liber Pontificalis*,
she did about fifty years later, in the time of Pope Celestine
(432).

From about that period we may date the beginnings of
what is commonly called "Gregorian Music," or more
correctly "Roman Chant" (*Cantilena Romana*). For it
may now be considered an established fact that while to
S. Gregory alone belongs the credit of having compiled,
arranged, and (in part) composed the Sacramentary and
Antiphoner, *i.e.* what we should now call the Missal and
Gradual, containing the words and music of the Mass, with
all its variable adjuncts of Introit, Gradual, Alleluia, Tract,

Offertory and Communion; on the other hand, the Choir Office-Book or *Liber Responsalis*, which contained the Antiphons, Psalm-tones and Responds, and which we *now* call the Antiphoner, ought more properly to be ascribed not to one, but to a series of Popes, beginning probably with S. Damasus, and including SS. Leo, Gelasius, Symmachus, John, Boniface, and finally S. Gregory.   That the Ambrosian music was largely laid under contribution in the formation cf this *répertoire* of Chants, which we will call the *Cantilena Romana*, is evident to anyone who will take the trouble to compare MSS. of the two uses, where the same words are set to music.   Two examples of Antiphons thus compared will be found on p. (11) of the examples (Ex. *Posuerunt* and *Benedictus*), and their number might easily be multiplied.

This *Cantilena Romana* then may be said to have reached its zenith with S. Gregory, who may probably have added to and codified it, towards the end of the 6th century; and the two centuries which followed might be justly called its "golden age."

It was this *Cantilena Romana* which our own S. Augustin brought over with him to England in 596.   It was this same "Roman Chant" which S. Benet Biscop, when he was on pilgrimage at Rome in 679, asked for and obtained for his Monastery at Wearmouth; it was this identical music which S. Wilfrid of York introduced into his Cathedral about the same time.   It was this same music which was enjoined at the 3rd Council of Cloveshoo (747) to be used throughout the Church of England.

We may then fairly infer that the music which we find in our early English Choro-liturgical MSS., and which is, it may be remarked, essentially the same as that in the MSS. of Italy, France and Germany, (allowing, of course, for additions made in later times), is the veritable old "Roman Chant."

Now to come to the practical part of our subject.   Pages (1) to (6) contain the Psalm-Tones in their order as given in the *Tonale secundum Usum Sarum*.

There are only two copies of this *Tonale* existing. Both
are in MS., one of the xivth Century in the Cathedral
Library at Salisbury (MS. 175), the other of the xvth Century
in the British Museum (Arundel MSS. 130), and in both
cases they form an Appendix to a *Directorium Chori*. But
earlier exemplars are to be found in the treatises of Walter de
Odington (1228) and Simon Tunstede (c. 1300), (both of them
English Monks and Musicians), reprinted by Coussemaker
in his "Scriptores." These give all the subjoined forms but
one, though not in the same order ; so we may fairly con-
jecture that the Sarum *Tonale* is co-eval with the Sarum
Breviary, and, as *that* was to all intents and purposes textually
identical with the old (unreformed) Roman Breviary, the same
may be said of the music.

But it must not be supposed that the *Tonale* is merely a
list of Tones with their endings and nothing more. For just
as, in the Antiphonal *method of singing*, the words of the Psalm
were intertwined with the Antiphon, so it was with their
music ; the Psalm-tone and ending were inseparably connected
with, and entirely dependent on, the music of the Antiphon.
A Psalm-tone by itself, without the music of its Antiphon, is,
if the simile may be allowed, something like a snail without
its shell.

Up to the 8th and 9th centuries, we know on the testimony
of contemporary writers (*e.g.* Amalarius) that the Antiphon
was still sung (as it probably had been from the first) between
every verse, or two, of the Psalm. This method was gradually
discontinued, and generally gave place to the use of singing
it before and after the Psalm only ; later still to the custom
(which we find in the Sarum books) of singing only the
first few words before the Psalm as a clue to the Tone and
ending. But the old custom has left its traces here and
there, as may be seen from the examples of Psalmody given
on pp. (11) and (12) of the examples, and others are still to
be found in the *Pontificale*.

To return to the *Tonale*. Its contents were these—It
went through the Modes in order. First it gave the ordinary

range of the mode, shewing by how many notes above or
below that range it was allowable for melodies in that
particular mode to go. Then it gave the different notes on
which a melody might begin. Then the number of tone-
endings (or "differences" as they were called) both of the
ordinary Psalm and Canticle Tones, and also of the Introit
forms. Then it proceeded to shew the connection between
the opening phrase of the Antiphon (technically called the
"variation") and the ending of the tone; *e.g.* it would shew
that an Antiphon in Mode I. beginning like *Posuerunt*, on
p. (11) *must* be followed by I. 1, and so through all the varieties
of the initial phrase of the Antiphon ; so that a Choir who
were properly instructed in the *Tonale*, as soon as they heard
the first notes of the Antiphon precented, would never be at
any loss to know what tone and ending were to follow.

There are two or three things in the Tone-table that it
may be worth while to point out—(1) That no less than five
of the endings are Ambrosian pure and simple, viz., I. 1.
III. 4 and 5. IV. 6. and VIII. 1., while others no doubt
might be traced to the same source. (2) That certain
endings (such as I. 6 and 7., III. 3., IV. 2, 3, and 5., V. 2.,
and VIII. 4) are evidently extensions of simpler ones, and
that, merely for the sake of "dove-tailing" into the Antiphon,
and it is evident that they point to the time when the
Antiphon was sung between every verse. Take, for instance,
I. 6 and 7. These are clearly varieties of the 5th ending, and
according to Joannes de Muris, (1370) are of Gallican origin.
Similarly IV. 2 and 3 are varieties of IV. 1. In the *Asperges*
the 1st ending is used for the verses of the Psalm, because it
fits in with the initial phrase of the Antiphon ; but at the end,
where only the *latter* half of the Antiphon is repeated, the
2nd ending is introduced in order to meet it. (See p. (12) of
examples.) In the same way it will be seen that IV. 5 is an
extension of IV. 4., V. 2. of V. 1., and VIII. 4. of VIII. 1.

It is a question whether any of these endings should be
used for the Psalms now-a-days, except perhaps at the end

of the Gloria (as in the case of the *Asperges*, mentioned above), where the Antiphon immediately follows; or when, in default of that, the Organist plays a similar phrase, in order to end on the final of the Mode. They might more legitimately be used for the Gospel Canticles, where the Intonation would occur in every verse. We may here note that as a rule the simplest forms were used for the Psalms of the ordinary weekdays.

A word more on some of the other endings. Tone II. 2 was reserved almost exclusively for what are called the Great O's. Tone III. 3 was used only once in the course of the year, and then to a Gospel Canticle. It is obvious that it would be intolerable if sung to the Psalms, since the interval between its final note and the dominant immediately following is a 7th! Tone III. 6. is certainly much more ancient (occurring in this form in the *Tonalia* of Odo, and Guido of Arezzo,) than the form usually met with—

do   do   do   la   do.si.la   sol

e . u . o . u . a . e

which cannot, we believe, boast an older parentage than that of Guidetti in the 16th century. Tone IV. 7 demands a word of notice, because it is not only in itself a relic of Ambrosianism, but is only used with an Ambrosian form of Antiphon, one of those cases where the dominant and final are identical, an irregularity which some of our modern purists would like to abolish. Of V. 3, that ending so dear to the lover of modern tonality, who congratulates himself on getting a melody in F major, we have merely to say that though it is in the Tone-Table (it does not occur in Walter de Odington's *Tonale*, but does in that of Simon Tunstede) it is never once used in the Sarum Antiphoner; it does however occur *once* in that of York, with that well-known Antiphon by Herman Contract *Alma Redemptoris*. Those who are familiar with the pathetic story in Chaucer's "Prioresses Tale" may perhaps be interested to know the actual melody which the "little clergion" learnt by rote in honour of "our blissful Ladye, Christës mother dear." (See page (15).)

Before we leave the subject of Tones and their endings,
attention may be drawn to two very uncommon and beautiful
forms which occur in the Sarum *Processionale*, and which were
used at the Procession to and from the Font on Easter Day
at Vespers.   They are the only relics left of Alleluiatic
Psalmody, *i.e.* of Psalms in which an Alleluia was intercalated
at the end of each verse.   (Pss. *Laudate pueri*, p. (12), and
In exitu, p. (13)).

And now we come to the question, How best to adapt
the Psalm-tones to English words?   It is with some
diffidence that we enter on this part of the subject, for, not to
mention living editors of Gregorian Psalters, we cannot be
unmindful of the works of those devout, earnest-minded
labourers in this field who have passed away.   The names of
Dyce, Oakley, Heathcote, Helmore, Shaw, Sargent, Raven-
shaw, and Monk are more or less familiar to us all.   It might
seem presumptuous to differ from these and other authorities,
were it not for one consoling thought, viz. that they all differ
among themselves.   " Every one of them has a psalm, and
every one of them has a doctrine" as to the method of
pointing it.   The question as to the best method is still a
matter for discussion.

A specimen of the system adopted in the lately-published
" Sarum Psalter" is shown on page (13).   The use of figures
to indicate the pointing is not new.   It has for some years
past found favour in Germany, but it is now for the first
time applied to the English Psalter, and serves a double
purpose not hitherto attainable ; (1) It provides for the
requirements of Religious houses, where the regular employ-
ment of Antiphons demands the use of a system by which
any Psalm can be sung to any Tone, and (2) in places
where Antiphons are not used, it leaves a Choirmaster at
liberty to choose his own tone and ending,—an obvious
advantage in the case of country choirs.

The system is really a simple one.   There are eight figures,
each answering to one of the eight Tones.   Each figure is

placed above the syllable on which the mediation and ending of its corresponding Tone begin, *i.e.* the first syllable on which the reciting note is left. The Tone being once chosen and learnt, the singer has nothing to do but to attend to its corresponding figure; all the other figures being, for the time, disregarded.

The pointing is based entirely on the Latin rules, as explained in the paper on Structure. Editors of other Psalters who have followed systems of pointing due to the gradual corruption of plainsong on the Continent will probably disapprove of the revival of the old rules, whether for Latin or English, and objections will no doubt be raised by those who say that the "genius of the English Language" requires certain modifications of rules which were intended for Latin only. But what is it in the English language which seems to them to demand this modification? It is undoubtedly the preponderance of monosyllables. It is the frequent recurrence of these as the final syllables of both mediation and ending, which, objectors say, necessitates a departure from the Latin rules. Now we would ask such objectors to examine the Latin Psalter a little more carefully. They will find a *very considerable number* of monosyllables occurring at the end of both mediation and cadence. And how are they treated? Page (14) of examples will shew. In the mediations of Tones 3 and 7, if it is necessary to the genius of the English language, as some appear to have thought, to chant

do   re   do   do   si.do
re   fa   mi   mi   re.mi
thy júdg - ments are right,

it must be equally necessary to that of the Latin to sing

do   re   do   do   si.do
re   fa   mi   mi   re.mi
le - tá - bi - tur réx.

The cases are perfectly analogous.

So, too, *Lord lift thou up* and *This I had* find their parallels in *Qui facit hæc* and *Dilexi.* In cases of this sort, where the number of·syllables was insufficient for the notes of the mediation, the old plain-chantists preferred to abbreviate the mediation rather than slur two notes together.

Or take the next instance—the abbreviated mediations of Tones 2, 4, 5, and 8. The Latin rule (which admits of no exception) requires the abbreviated forms of mediation in these Tones to be used in the case of all monosyllables and Hebrew names. Oh, but (objectors say) there are some cases in English, *e.g.* personal pronouns coming after a strong accent, either a verb or a preposition, which must be treated as enclitics. Why in English, when they are not so treated in Latin? If it is not contrary to the genius of the Latin tongue to sing *quis est, E-phrá-ta, con-trí-tus est,'* it cannot be contrary to the genius of the English language to sing *a-gainst him, con-cér-ning me.* Besides, if we once began to make exceptions, there would be no knowing where to stop. We could not limit enclitically-treated words to personal pronouns. We should be obliged to extend the list of exceptions to every case where the penultimate syllable is more strongly accented than the final syllable, like *hárts' feet,* or *púre words*; yet it would be absurd to say that *feet* and *words* were enclitic.

Apropos of this point, we may quote the words of the late Mr. Dyce, who is generally acknowledged to be an authority on Plain Chant. Speaking of examples of this nature, he says " In the great majority of cases the words "are best enunciated by the Latin mode; and even of the "exceptions made by Marbeck, there is scarcely one which "we can positively affirm to be of necessity an exception ; so "that, on the whole, it appears advisable to adhere to the "Latin rule, and to place the rise of tone uniformly on the "last monosyllable." (Dyce, *Preface and Appendix to the Book of Common Prayer, 1844.*)

And the Latin rules equally apply to *endings.* There is no more reason for pointing *re-frésh-ed my sóul,* or *the ín-no-cent blóod* than for *vi-ví-fi-ca me,* or *ro-bo-rá-bi-tur vir.* And the same remark applies to the special treatment of

the endings of Tones 4, 6 and 8, when the strong accent lies on the fourth syllable from the end, followed by two weak syllables and a final monosyllable. The English examples here given are in absolute agreement with the Latin, and cases of a similar kind might be multiplied in both languages to almost any extent.

In conclusion it may be worth while to notice that the Psalm-tones were never intended for instrumental accompaniment. Where it is deemed necessary to accompany them, (i.) a strict attention to their modality should be observed, and (ii.) common chords, and chords of the first inversion only should be employed as a rule, with a judicious use of passing notes and suspensions. There is no need, however, to enlarge upon this subject, as it is fully discussed under " *Accompaniment.*"

HYMNODY.

The current views and use of hymns in Church services to-day differ very widely from those of mediæval and early times.

In Western Christendom metrical hymns were only admitted to the public services slowly and under great restrictions, for it was held more fit and proper to keep to the Psalter and the biblical Canticles, with a small number of others, such as the *Te Deum, Sanctus, Gloria in excelsis,* which might almost claim to be biblical.

This reverential feeling was first broken down in the enthusiasm caused by the hymns of St. Hilary and St. Ambrose: hymn-singing, which till their time had been practised only outside the churches, then began to enter into them under the stress of religious differences, and under the shelter especially of the great name of St. Ambrose: but it was reserved for St. Benet nearly 150 years later first to secure it a formal place in public worship. Others were not slow to follow his example when once set, and very quickly hymns began to be a recognised part of the Divine Office throughout the West, though the traditional conservatism of the city of Rome continued to exclude them till the end of the 12th century. But though the hymns had taken their place in the Divine Office, still nearly four more centuries were to elapse before non-biblical hymns were at all generally admitted at Mass, and then the Proses or Sequences came in only as it were by a side door (see below p. 72): once admitted they enjoyed great popularity up to the 16th century, but then once again, even in countries where the Latin Mass was retained, the tide of feeling turned so much against them that at the revision of the Roman Missal in 1570 only four of them were retained. So jealously have their progress and growth been watched and checked.

A second point to notice is that both Hymns and
Sequences were used till the Reformation in a fixed cycle
more or less peculiar to the local ' use ' : there was no more
liberty of choice in this respect than in respect of psalms,
lessons, or collects.

On both these points the modern English view of hymns
is in sharp contrast with the old.

So far from being organized on a fixed cycle they are now
not authoritatively organized at all, but are mere unauthorized
interpolations into our services, and often alas! chosen with
very little system at all.

But though unauthorized they are extremely popular, and
in fact tend to usurp the place and care that should be
bestowed on the authorized musical parts of the services—the
Kyrie, Credo, Sanctus, and *Gloria,* or the Psalms and Canticles.

The great activity which has been displayed since Reformation times in the composition of hymns in English, and the
great successes which have been achieved in this field, have
caused the old Latin hymns([1]) to relinquish by degrees the
monopoly which they once enjoyed, but they still are the
most important part of our hymnody and it is with them only
that we are concerned here.

The first group consists of the Hymns proper, written for
use in the choir-offices and principally for Evensong, Mattins,
and Lauds.

1. The metres employed vary very considerably : that in
which St. Ambrose himself wrote—the iambic tetrameter,
better known now as Long Measure—is however by far the
commonest, and for practical purposes at the present time
almost the only one available : others were tried with varying
success, and one or two instances of such hymns may be given
here before passing on to deal with the main block of Long
Measure hymns.

---

(1) It is convenient to group the later Latin Hymns of the 16th-18th
centuries with the old ones as keeping the old language and a good deal of that
restrained dogmatic spirit which is characteristic of the early Latin hymns.

For these four-line verses some of the lyric metres were employed: of these the most useful proved to be the Sapphic, of which there are 13 hymns and 9 melodies included in the Sarum Hymnal: a specimen is given on page (20), No. 16. For other instances here, as elsewhere, reference must be made to *Plainsong Hymn Melodies*: see the Sapphic melodies Nos. 18, 44, 55–59, 61.

Another popular lyrical metre was the Choriambic, of which two forms are found in the melodies of the Sarum Hymnal; the first consists of four equal lines of eleven syllables, and only appears for the hymn *O quam glorifica luce coruscas* (P.H.M., 66 : O.H.B. 89) : the second is 12, 12, 12, 8, and there are four melodies, set to either *Sacris solemniis juncta sint gaudia* for Corpus Christi, or the better known Martyrs' Hymn[1]

Sanctorum meritis inclita gaudia
Pangamus socii gestaque fortia:
Nam gliscit animus promere cantibus
Victorum genus optimum.

A very short acquaintance with either the Sapphic or this second Choriambic metre will convince an unbiassed mind of the possibilities for English Hymns which lie hid in them: some have already been successfully handled, though one of the best in diction, viz., that by Mr. Philip Pusey, "Lord of our Life and God of our Salvation," (H. A. & M. 214) is marred by the occurrence of the cæsura after unimportant words.

The metre 7, 7, 7, 7 occurs only once in the Sarum Hymnal in the cento from Prudentius, *Cultor dei memento:* another cento from the same is given in H. A. & M. as "Father most high be with us," but without the proper melody : this can be seen here on page (20) No. 13, and will at once attract any musician.

The very short metre 6, 6, 6, 6 claims two melodies (P.H.M. 63, 64), both for the hymn *Ave Maris Stella* ; and the long 12, 12, 12, 12 metre has also two melodies (P.H.M. 46, 47)

[1] See P.H.M. 45, 51-53.

which belong to the two hymns *Aurea luce* and *Annue Christe* ; this exhausts all the four-line hymns of the Sarum Hymnal apart from Long Measure.

Only one six-line metre is employed, and that is very familiar from such hymns as *Urbs beata* (Blessed city, heavenly Salem) and *Pange lingua* (Sing, my tongue, the glorious battle). The same is also used, with an additional line for chorus, by Prudentius in his well-known hymn *Corde natus* (Of the Father's love begotten), but for English authority for the use of this hymn one must go to York or Hereford.

The use of other lyric metres is very rare and need not be detailed here, but a word must be said on elegiac hymns. The best known of these are the processionals, *Salve festa dies* (Hail thee, Festival Day) and *Gloria laus et honor* (Glory and honour and laud) which are not strictly speaking hymns at all, though they may be roughly described as hymns with chorus : it was a form very well adapted for processions, and most popular there though not confined to them. The same metre was also employed for hymns proper in some few hymnals, *e.g.* the following hymn of the nuns of Barking—

> *Virgo dei genitrix quem totus non capit orbis,*
> *In tua se clausit viscera factus homo.*

but it never became popular and even the processional melodies, which did become extremely popular and almost universal, present considerable difficulties and need a great deal of care in performance.

We can now leave the less usual metres and turn to the hymns of the old Ambrosian type in Long Metre.

The earliest melodies no doubt were very simple, and many survive and are among the most popular. Some are literally syllabic and would have satisfied Cranmer's test of strict plainsong, as they have only one note to a syllable, (pp. (18), (19), Nos. 7, 11) : but the bulk of them are not quite so severe and have at intervals a single group of notes on a syllable instead of a single note. A third class, called *melismatic,* is more elaborate still and admits of more than one group of notes on a syllable, but these are comparatively rare : the most conspicuous instance in the Sarum Hymnal is the Ascension melody *Eterne rex altissime* (P.H.M. 41, and see above p. 52.)

Another point to be noticed is the construction of the melodies. Like most plainsong they circle round one note, but this note is not as a rule the *dominant*, as it is in that plainsong which has grown out of recitation in monotone, but more often it is the *final* of the mode. A reference to some of the examples will make this plain. In p. (19) No. 9 every line except one begins or ends on A : p. (18) No. 5 is a slightly more elaborate melody but it has the same characteristic recurrence of the Final in six out of the eight prominent positions.

Thirdly it is to be observed that the various lines of the melody are often closely related to one another : the commonest relationship is between the first and second line (pp. (19) (20), Nos. 10, 15): or between the first and the last line, (p. (19) Nos. 9, 12) : an interesting parallelism between the second and fourth line is given in p. (18) No. 5, a kind which is rare except when the first and third lines also are alike (as in P.H.M. 20) : it is still more rare for the third line to copy the second, but an instance is the third-mode Easter melody *Ad cenam Agni providi* (P.H.M. 39).

All these three points tell greatly in favour of the plainsong melodies: they are simple and their compass very small : it is almost impossible to go wrong because they circle so much round one note : and they are easy to learn and never forgotten because of the balance of the lines. The only drawback to them is that they are so largely unknown : more's the pity.

But it is now time to turn to the Sequences.

These do not begin to appear as part of Mass till the middle of the 9th century. There had then been recently developed a great taste for extending the Gregorian melodies by long cadences sung without words which were called by the name either of *jubilum, sequentia* or *neupma*. They rested on a very old basis for St. Austin bears witness to the entrancing effect of these *jubila*, but in the 8th and 9th centuries the fashion grew apace, and it became common to make such additions to many of the parts of the Church's song. Soon there arose a difficulty in remembering such long and elaborate melodies without words, and to help the memory attempts were made to fit in some words to the music.

Of all these *jubila* the most elaborate were those which followed the Alleluia at Mass; in fact they came to be a separate composition altogether from the Gregorian Alleluia. Some tentative efforts seem to have been made to supply them with words, but all hung fire until Notker Balbulus a monk of St. Gall (c. 860) took up the idea : it was suggested to him by the arrival at St. Gall of a monk of Jumiéges who had escaped from the pillage of his monastery by the Normans, bringing with him a service-book in which the *jubila* were partly fitted with words. Notker seized upon the notion and extended it by writing words for the whole of the *jubilum* : and receiving much encouragement in connexion with his first efforts, he went on and became the father of this branch of Hymnody.

Various names were given to these compositions. Sometimes they were called Proses from the fact that they were not metrical, while, in Germany especially, those which sprung from the Alleluia at Mass got the name of Sequence, as preluding the giving out of the Gospel in the regular formula " *Sequentia sancti Evangelii secundum . . . .*" A good example of the non-metrical Prose of the Notkerian type, though not by Notker, is the well-known Easter Sequence *Victimae paschali* (H.N. 28). Another good specimen is the early French Prose *Salus eterna* (see p. (21)).

Here the noticeable points of the Notkerian Prose stand out clearly, viz. (i) the freedom of the rhythm and (ii.) the repetition of each line of music so that the Prose mainly consists of pairs of parallel lines. The former Prose has also a special interest of its own in being a miniature music drama, and so linked on to the later Mystery Plays.

Having won for themselves a place in the Mass by this round-about method, Sequences became universally popular : new melodies soon were written for them, and when the poet was no longer tied to an already existing melody, sequences naturally fell into regular metrical form and lost the free rhythm characteristic of the early sequence.

The greatest master of metrical sequences was Adam of St. Victor (c. 1150) whose writings are poems of great force and beauty, but the melodies associated with them lack the rugged power and spontaneity of the old Proses. Not many of his proses found their way into England, though room was made for two of them in the Temporale of the Sarum Gradual, viz : *Zyma vetus* and *Lux jocunda* and others are found in other parts, *e.g.*, *Missus Gabriel de celis* (see p. (23)). A good instance of the metrical sequence is *Veni Sancte Spiritus* (Come thou Holy Paraclete) H.N. 84. P.M. xxxviii. (H. A. & M. 156) or the popular Christmas sequence *Letabundus.* H.N. 94.

The result of this process by which sequences became metrical was the breaking down of a great part of the distinction in structure between them and the hymns. Even a 12th (or 11th) century Prose like *Laudes deo devotas* (see p. (22)) has approximated somewhat to the hymn form, as is clearly seen in the constant repetition of the first line of the melody : later the approximation is far more complete *e.g.* in *Jesu dulcis memoria* (Jesu, the very thought is sweet) which, though originally a hymn, appears set as a sequence in the Sarum printed Graduals. H.N. 18. PM. xli. (H. A. & M. 177). Another instance is the *Dies irae* (Day of wrath! O day of mourning) which, so far as the words go, is a normal Sequence, but, so far as the melody goes, is more like a hymn tune which is three times repeated and then ended by a coda P.M. xliv. (H. A. & M. 398).[1] Partly from this and partly from other causes a crisis came in the history of the

---

(1) And H.N. 46. But there the construction is somewhat obscured : this is also true of the setting at the end of the Appendix of H. A. & M.

sequences: their popularity, which had outrun its powers, came to an end, and they disappeared from the Roman Missal almost entirely in the revisions of the 16th century.

In conclusion one or two practical points may be touched on.

First, with regard to Sequences, there is a great deal to be said for their revival[1]: it is true that they were a late development and that in the modern Roman Missal they are almost suppressed, but some singing is wanted between Epistle and Gospel, and it is in accordance with the *very earliest* and best traditions of the Church to separate lessons by singing just as we do habitually at Mattins and Evensong. Where the Gradual and Alleluia are still retained, as in the Missal, it is probably true that a sequence *besides* is as a rule undesirable, but where they are not, as in the Book of Common Prayer, there is more to be said for introducing hymnody at this point than at any other point of the Liturgy.

Secondly, with regard to the hymns in the Divine Office, it seems true to say that in these days, when emotional or subjective hymns are becoming more and more common, it is extremely advisable to reserve a place in the service for a more solid biblical or dogmatic hymn of the type of the old Latin hymns.

Such an "office hymn" seems now-a-days to be out of its place in the position which it occupied at Evensong or Lauds, that is before *Magnificat* or *Benedictus*, for the structure or (to speak more precisely), *articulation* of our Morning and Evening Services differs greatly from that of the Breviary Offices from which they were developed; but this objection does not extend to the position of the hymn at Mattins in the Breviary, where it stands between the *Venite* and the Psalms and gives to the whole service from its beginning onward the character appropriate to the season or festival. This position is still available and is *far* the best place that can be reserved for the office-hymn at our Mattins, and by analogy at Evensong. Liturgical

<hr>

(1) A series of Sequences for the year prepared for the Plainsong and Mediæval Music Society is now in the press.

precedent (¹) and practical considerations both point in the
same direction, for an office hymn is recognized to be of far
more practical value at the beginning of a service than when
it is nearly over.

Some modern hymnals definitely supply such a series of
Office Hymns, notably *The Hymnal Noted*, *The Hymner*,
and the *Office Hymn Book*: in others, and especially
Hymns Ancient and Modern, a very large number of such
hymns are included, but they are mixed up with modern and
subjective hymns, and care should be taken to select the
proper office hymns with the help of some such book as
Moorsom's *Historical Companion*.

Thirdly as to the melodies, it is a great pity when the
words and their proper melodies are divorced. In many cases
they can be traced back hand in hand for centuries, and
in some even to a common source; to divorce them now
is barbarous. But independently of the connexion of a definite
hymn with a definite melody, there is considerable incongruity
in singing an old Latin hymn to a modern melody. The
confusion of styles is quite inartistic and jars: it produces
something of the same effect as a beautiful Gothic cross
flanked by two Renaissance candlesticks, and in some cases
the incongruity is even greater, and as monstrous as would be
the dome of St. Paul's Cathedral set upon the top of West-
minster Abbey. Unfortunately in a large number of the
translations of Latin hymns in *Hymns Ancient and Modern*,
the original metre has not been retained: in this way the
use of the old melody or even in many cases of *any* old
plainsong melody is made impossible. This is much to be
deplored ; but at any rate, in all cases where it is possible,
the old melody should be retained.(²)

(¹) The evidence of Prime, Terce, Sext, and None reinforces that of Mattins,
and for the same position at Evensong there is the authority of the Ambrosian
Breviary. There is neither precedent nor authority for putting it in place of
" the anthem."

(²) It is much to be desired that in any new edition of *Hymns Ancient and
Modern* the Compilers will include everywhere the old melodies where they can
still be used ; pending that good move, a reference may perhaps be allowed to the
present writer's collection called *The Plainsong Melodies of Hymns Ancient and
Modern*, in which an attempt is made to supply the deficiency.

Fourthly as to the method of performance. The difficulties are here less than in any part of plainsong because the words have a very definite metre (or at least rhythm), and the music follows that metre exactly, and as a rule very simply. The great mistake is to imagine that the single notes are of equal length because they look alike : it is more true to say that no two notes are of the same length, any more than any two syllables of a line of poetry have exactly the same value. *Follow implicitly the metre or rhythm of the words :* this is the simple rule and the only one : the performance should be as much as possible like the recitation of a good elocutionist, only with the pitch and inflections of the voice musically defined. It follows that where two notes occur on a syllable they will be roughly speaking half the length that a single note would have on the same syllable, *e.g. Rector potens verax deus* must keep the same natural rhythm of the words whether it be monotoned, or sung to (p. (19) No. 9) syllabically or to (p. (19) No. 10) where the fourth, fifth and sixth syllables will each have two notes : the three groups of double notes will only have the same time-value as the corresponding single notes because *the time-value of any note or group is determined absolutely by the syllable to which it is sung.* When two or three notes occur to a syllable it is not difficult to give the note-group the rhythmical value of the single syllable to all intents and purposes by placing the strong accent on the first of the group : in more extended neums it is possible that the opening notes, especially if ascending, (*e.g.* in *Eterne rex altissime* P.H.M. 41, and see p. 52 above) should be treated as appoggiatura.

Where organ accompaniment is required—the hymns are often better without—it should be *very unobtrusive* with only very rare use of pedals and it should slavishly follow (not lead) the rhythm of the singing. The harmonies used should be *modal* and the parts should be as stationary as possible so as to leave all possible freedom of rhythm to the melody.([1])

([1]) The harmonies in Hymnal Noted fail often in both these respects, but those provided for the Office Hymn Book are extremely well done, and others are in preparation to accompany the 'Plainsong Hymn Melodies.'

In conclusion it is to be hoped both that the old Latin plainsong hymns and melodies may be given more of their due place, and that modern hymns, however beautiful, may be more kept in their place and not allowed to encroach on either their *confrères* or, what is still more important, on the authorized and prescribed musical parts of the Prayer Book. Hymns have a great value and power, and this would be the last place in which to decry them, but there is something upside-down in the state of mind which is willing to *say*, or even gabble, all the proper musical parts of the service—the Psalms and Canticles, or the *Kyrie, Credo, Sanctus,* and *Gloria* —and then interpolate a hymn somewhere 'to brighten up the service a bit.' First let the services as they stand in the Prayer Book be rendered musically with all the care and art available, and then afterwards there will be a place for putting in hymns, and as well a justification for doing so which otherwise is wanting. And among hymns and hymn-tunes those surely have a first claim, which come to us hallowed by the associations and devotion of generations.

MUSIC OF THE HOLY EUCHARIST

The English Order of Holy Communion prescribes the use, wherever it is possible, of a considerable amount of music. It is most desirable that the rubrical demands should be loyally satisfied in this respect first, before anything else. It may be desirable to introduce additions to the minimum of music contemplated by the Prayer Book, and there is a great deal to be said for reviving where possible the Offices, Graduals &c., which have behind them the authority of almost universal use in the West,—much less to be said, except on the score of popularity and convenience, for introducing hymns,—but this should always come second to the proper execution of the music which is prescribed in the Book of Common Prayer.

This latter falls into two heads ; (i) part of the chant is simple recitative such as the Preface, or the Lord's Prayer : (ii) part, such as *the Creed*, the *Kyrie, Sanctus, Gloria*, is more developed melody.

i. (*a*) The music of the Preface and of the Versicles which lead up to it from the *Sursum Corda* according to the use of the English Prayer Book, or from *The Lord be with you* according to the old use still retained in the Scottish and American Liturgies, is of extreme antiquity, and whatever else is sung to modern music, it is desirable here to keep to the old chant.

The booke of Common Praier noted of John Merbecke (1550)—the only printed musical counterpart of the Prayer Book put forth at the Reformation—here fails to give help : the words are all set in monotone, no doubt because Merbecke felt that the music could not be forced to submit to the limitation which apparently governed his adaptation, viz. that there should never be more than one note assigned to a syllable. The instructions given him by Cranmer for a syllabic chant

were doubtless caused by the corrupt rendering at that time of
the melismatic plainsong, which made it as unsuitable for
congregational worship as the florid masses in polyphonic
music, which came into vogue during the 15th century and
were forbidden in Elizabeth's Injunctions. The old chant is
found in several forms which vary to a considerable degree :
it is a great pity that in many places foreign and debased
versions have been adopted instead of the English ones, which
are simpler and intrinsically better, besides having a strong
claim on our allegiance. The Sarum version has however
been several times adapted to English words, and may be
found best in *Notes on Ceremonial*,[1] with the rest of the
recitative music prescribed in the Communion Office of the
Prayer Book. *Choir Responses according to the Use of Sarum*
(Novello 1894) contains all that is necessary for choirs.

This whole section closing with the Preface forms one
continuous musical piece, and serves as the introduction
to the *Sanctus*: it is therefore very important that musically
it should lead naturally into it without any pause or hitch.
The Preface may be taken as having either *do* or *fa* as its
reciting note, and the various plainsong chants of the *Sanctus*
will fit on naturally to one or other of these alternatives : but
care must be taken that if the Preface and *Sanctus* are not
sung at the normal pitch, but transposed for convenience to
some higher or lower key, they should both be transposed
alike.

For example with Merbecke's (1st mode) *Sanctus* it is
best to look upon the Preface as having *fa* for its reciting
note ; it will then lead naturally into the *Sanctus*: but if the
priest wishes to recite at a higher pitch, say on G, both
Preface and *Sanctus* must be transposed a note higher: if on
A, two notes higher: and so on, and the same transposition
will affect the *whole* music from the versicles which lead up
to the Preface to the end of the *Sanctus* or *Benedictus*. When

<hr>

[1] Pickering & Chatto 1888 (the music is reprinted under the title *Ritual Music*, price 1/-). See also the *Altar Book* (Percival 1894).

the *Sanctus* is sung to a modern composition, it is probably best that the reciting note of the Preface should be taken as either the key note or the fourth degree of the scale of the *Sanctus* : there is bound to be an awkward hiatus in the transition from the ancient modal music to music in the modern scale, and it is perhaps best to bridge it over in this way. When the Preface is sung unaccompanied, as it always should be, the awkwardness will be minimized : and if it is accompanied the last notes should not be so harmonized as to lead into the *Sanctus* by a full close ; for this would be very alien to the spirit of the plain chant however agreeable to modern ears.

b. The Lord's Prayer presents no such difficulties as it is an independent melody, complete in itself.

c. The Sarum tones to the Collect, Epistle, and Gospel, are much to be preferred to the modern Roman ones which have been adopted in many places : full directions will be found in the books quoted above. As a practical point it should be remembered that these are reading-inflections not melodies and the " singing " should not be full round singing, still less clumsy and laboured, but quite natural and unobtrusive and as much like melodious reading as possible.

d. In many churches it is customary to sing the Comfortable Words. The wisdom of this must be gravely questioned : first because (as is clear from the Order of the Communion of 1548) they are closely linked on to the Confession and Absolution—a connexion in which the use of music is of doubtful expediency : secondly because singing at this point tends to obscure the prominence which the *Sursum Corda* (or *The Lord be with you*) ought to have, as being the starting point of the central part of the Liturgy. The music to which they are commonly sung is nothing else but an attempt at adapting them to a lesson-tone, but based on foreign models and ill carried out.

ii. (*a*) The melodies of the *Kyrie* present a considerable difficulty because our modern words and use vary so much

G

from the old system of *Kyrie eleison* sung nine times consecutively. The Sarum *Kyries* are all arranged more or less elaborately in 3 sets of 3 each: it is still possible to keep to this arrangement, but (except in a few cases where the old 9th *Kyrie* is so elaborated as to be practically a double one) something extra has then to be provided for the 10th Commandment. Merbecke is here no help at all, for the ninefold *Kyrie* was still retained when his book appeared, and while it is possible (though difficult) to adapt the long melodies of the Sarum Gradual to our response[1] it is totally impossible to adapt Merbecke's note-for-syllable melody to it. What is now sung as Merbecke's *Kyrie* owes merely its first seven notes to him and the rest is a modern addition, due to Mr. William Dyce.

(*b*) The Creed has one melody[2] that preeminently belongs to it and for hundreds of years was the only one in use: it belongs, so far as simplicity goes, to the class of recitative rather than that of melody. Merbecke seems to have despaired of adapting it to English words[3] and preferred to write a melody of his own which though of considerable melodic beauty lacks the simplicity and repose of the old melody. Either of these is well suited (the old melody preeminently so) for congregational use at the present day.

(*c*) Of the *Sanctus* a good deal has already been said: all the melodies for it (two in Merbecke and ten in the Sarum Gradual) are simple and effective.

---

[1] The Plainsong and M. M. Society are on the point of issuing a complete English *Ordinarium Missæ* (*Kyries, Glorias, Credo, Sanctus and Agnus*) which has been long preparing, on the basis of the Sarum Gradual but with due regard to foreign versions of the same melodies. Meanwhile it may be noted that Messrs. Masters have published for the Society the *Missa Rex Splendens* and *the Creed* carefully adapted from English authorities. This is much to be preferred to debased French Plainsong Masses such as the *Missa de Angelis*, *Missa Regia* etc.

[2] See *Missa Rex Splendens*.

[3] Attempts had been made to adapt it to English words before Merbecke's time (see Brit: Mus: Add. MSS. 34191 which contains a very interesting adaptation of the plainchant of the Mass to an English version prior to the Prayer Book of 1549.

(*d*) The *Gloria in excelsis* no longer stands in its old position and it has been altered by the repetition of the clause "(*Thou*) *that takest away the sins of the world, have mercy upon us*": but neither of these changes seriously affects it musically. Merbecke's setting is in many ways good, but will not compare for simplicity and grandeur with the old 4th mode setting which is a fit pendant to the Creed, or even with the popular 6th mode setting of the Sarum Gradual.

Two parts of the *Ordinarium Missæ* have so far not been mentioned but are reserved to the end, because they are not prescribed by the present Prayer Book, though both were prescribed in 1549 and appear therefore in Merbecke.

The *Benedictus* is simply the last two sentences of the *Sanctus* and belongs to it entirely; if sung at all it should be sung as part of it, not as a separate interpolation.

The *Agnus Dei* is a separate thing: its place in our service has been sufficiently vindicated lately: musically it presents no difficulties.

Before proceeding further it seems advisable to emphasize strongly the simple character of all the foregoing music. The whole of the Gregorian system of music for the Holy Eucharist goes on the assumption that the chants of the *Ordinarium Missæ*, especially those of the *Credo, Sanctus, Agnus*, and *Gloria*, are of a simple character—are in fact congregational. This is one great reason among many others for preferring the old Gregorian plainsong to modern compositions, which are as a rule possible at best only to the choir, and not always to them.

The elaborate plainsong is connected not with the invariable parts of the Liturgy but with the variable parts—Offices, Graduals, Alleluias, etc.—which, though varying much among themselves[1] in difficulty, are all of them more exacting than the melodies of the invariable parts.

We have no longer any variable parts of the Liturgy prescribed in our Prayer Book except the Collects, Epistles

---

[1] In the main because the parts sung by solo voices are markedly more difficult than those assigned to the body of the choir.

and Gospels, which are only in a very restricted sense musical ;
so we have no *obligations* in the way of music beyond those
already mentioned.

In some churches it may be possible and advisable to
revive (under episcopal sanction) large parts, if not the whole,
of the music of the variables *De tempore* and *De sanctis*,
Offices, Graduals, etc. ; but such churches can never be
more than a few. There are probably however many
churches where something of the sort might be done. In the
Prayer Book of 1549 and in Merbecke we have a series of
Offices for the year and a selected number of Offertories and
Post Communions : but these Offices are merely psalms, and
even as a series of psalms have very few points of contact
with the Gregorian series and are no improvement at all on
the old. There is however a great deal to be said for singing
a psalm or portion of a psalm at the Office and at the
Communion. It was a great loss when in the middle ages
the psalm entirely, or almost entirely, dropped out in these
places, leaving merely the Antiphon at the Communion, and at
the Office the Antiphon with one verse of the psalm and the
Gloria. If we cannot have both psalm and antiphon at the Office
(*i.e.* Introit) we can at all events have the former which is the
more important, and could be easily restored.   Where that is
done, the series of the Gregorian scheme would be an obvious
line to follow for the Offices in bringing back the old custom
of perhaps 1500 years' standing of ' coming before His
presence with a psalm.'

The present rubric in our Prayer Book as to Offertories
does not provide expressly for their being sung, as the rubric
in the Prayer Book of 1549 did: but the sentences *are*
commonly sung, though rarely, if ever, to the Merbecke
melodies. Many of these are on the ancient lines and of
considerable merit, and it seems a great pity that they should
be so neglected as they usually are.

If the custom of singing a psalm during the Communion
is to be revived it is a little more difficult to see what line

should be followed. In old days the usual thing was to finish the psalm which had been begun at the Office but stopped when the celebrant was ready to begin ; and this may still be advisable. But at other times a special psalm was sung connected with the Communion-anthem or appropriated to the day, *e.g.* the psalms of the early part of the psalter were sung consecutively on the week days of Lent. In either case it would be possible to sing a psalm and one of Merbecke's Post Communions with it as its antiphon, and so approximate still more closely to the old system.

Thus in these three places, Office, Offertory, and Communion, a good deal may be done in a simple way on Merbecke's lines to make up for the want of a *proprium* in the Book of Common Prayer, and to use the psalms, as above all they ought to be used, in connexion with eucharistic worship.

ACCOMPANIMENT.

The question of the proper accompaniment for plainsong is a very vexed one. It is always difficult to add on to a masterpiece, and this is exactly the difficulty which the accompanist of plainsong has to face: his work is more a question of delicate taste than of principle; he must be in thorough *rapport* with the chant, taking it as sung in its palmiest days, and must add only what harmonizes closely with its genius, and just so much as will give the needful support and no more—in short he must be sympathetic and unobtrusive.

But though the success of plainsong accompaniment depends on such rare qualities of taste, it does at the same time rest upon principles.   There are four alternative theories possible with regard to accompaniment.   (i.) The extreme purist would reject it altogether: on the other hand (ii.) the extreme vandal would deck it out with all the resources of the modern harmonic system.   First a word about each of these views, which are the opposite poles of opinion, and then we shall probably find that the true solution of the question lies between the two.

(i.) The extreme purist is theoretically unassailable. When plainsong was at its zenith, it was always sung unaccompanied : moreover practically there is a good deal to be said for his contention when dealing with either a very *small* or a very *large* body of voices.   In both these cases it is probably best to have no accompaniment : but with the ordinary choir most people will prefer to use an organ accompaniment, partly as a support to the voices, and partly also to give, as it were, a background to the chant.   In the old days there was no theoretical objection to accompaniment—in fact musicians were in too great a hurry in availing themselves of crude organs, and the faultiness of their instruments and performers in the 11th and 12th centuries no doubt did much to ruin plainsong singing; but that is no reason why we, with better instruments and more skill available, should not make use of them, if only we can do so without mutilating and spoiling the melodies or their rendering.

(ii.) The extreme vandal on the other hand has nothing to back him. If he wishes to use in Church-worship all the resources of modern harmony, by all means let him do so; there is plenty of good music written for the purpose: but let him keep clear of plainsong. Nature and Art equally abhor a hybrid, and *chromatic plainsong* is a mere hybrid, the offspring often of Gregorian or High Church tendencies on the part of the parson, coupled with a limited knowledge of merely modern music on the part of the Organist and Choir,—pleasing neither, and intrinsically abominable.

But when it is agreed that plainsong shall be accompanied, and that its accompaniment shall be written according to the ancient modal system—for that is what it comes to—the question is not yet at an end. The modal system reigned supreme for a long period, and throughout that period underwent considerable modifications, and we have still to decide which era represents the system at its best for the purpose of serving as a model for accompaniments to-day. The history of modal harmony falls into two divisions—(iii.) the strict period which lasted to the end of the 12th century, and (iv.) the free period which culminated in Palestrina.

In the early period all harmony was as strictly diatonic as the melodies were: the only accidental permissible was the Bb, in fact no other *black note* existed: the laws of progression were of course rudimentary and the permissible concords few. These were the weaknesses of the system, while its strength lay in the fact that it was strictly modal and introduced no note which was out of the mode.

・ At the end of the 12th century we begin to hear for the first time of this modal purity being tampered with: other accidentals make their first appearance in the harmonies. The name for them (*musica ficta* or *falsa*) shews clearly the way in which they were regarded. At first only two additional accidentals were tolerated, the E♭ and the F♯,[1] and it was some considerable time before the chromatic principle was extended further than this. [2]

No one but the most intolerant antiquary could regret the innovation, it was a necessary step on the way to the glories of modern harmony : but at the same time it cannot be denied that it was the beginning of the downfall of the modal system. Harmonic gain was modal loss ; and the harmony of Palestrina's time, though too antiquated for many musicians of to-day, would have been too novel for the singers of the palmy days of plainsong. They would have asked why if the melody was to be kept strictly in the mode the parts should be allowed to go outside it ; and they would have a good deal of justice on their side, for the new licenses tended to spoil the tonality and break down the distinctions between the modes, and even, as the event proved, to destroy the modes themselves.

If we have to decide then between the strict and the free system of modal harmony, we choose the former as being in absolute accord with the melody (which is of the essence of good accompaniment), whereas the latter harmonizes less with it by admitting notes which are foreign to both melody and mode. We are not bound to the weaknesses of the strict period—its crude progressions for example which are only accidental to it ; but we shall do well to keep to that which is of its essence and is its strength, viz. the strict adherence to elementary concords and to the diatonic notes of the mode.

---

[1] The sign ♯ however was not invented till the xvth century : till then only the b molle ♭ and the b quadratum ♮ were in vogue and the last name did duty for the ♯.

[2] The extent to which strict diatonic harmony was cultivated has hitherto been much under-estimated. Few specimens of this work are accessible in modern books but a good deal exists in MSS. and ought to be published in facsimile. The principle however is clear that until chromatic variation was admitted, chromatic harmony was impossible : and this principle still holds good for diatonic melody.

One special point which is crucial with regard to the two systems deserves further discussion *i.e.* the cadences.

The whole conception of a 'leading note' is foreign to the strict modal system : it is only possible in two out of the eight modes, and those two were the least used. This seems not to have been a mere accident but due to a definite dislike of the leading note in a close, for in the fifth mode the E is usually avoided, and in the sixth mode where this policy becomes almost impossible, it is not uncommon to find the whole melody transposed a fifth higher so as to be able by the use of B♭ to avoid a semitonal close.

The reason of this is not very far to seek, for from the point of view of *melody* a semitonal close is very indeterminate and unsatisfying. We are entirely accustomed to it now, and can hardly avoid mentally harmonizing it and so clothing its nakedness, but any one who has sung much without accompaniment will nevertheless often have felt how weak it is melodically, compared to the strong cadence which rises from a flat seventh to the Final.[1] How then is it that this is now solely archaic ?

The whole musical instinct as to closes has been turned round, and this conversion is purely due to harmony. Though a semitonal cadence is melodically weak, when harmonized as a full close it is immensely strong, for it brings into clear contrast the two sharply distinguished chords of the dominant and the tonic, and nothing else serves so completely to determine the tonality of the melody, *i.e.* nothing else makes so satisfying a close. No wonder that the perfect cadence, once invented, took musicians by storm : they revelled in it and almost worked it to death : it was in greatest vogue in the 16th century and has probably since then been on the decline, though it still enjoys over-much popularity.

In the light of this piece of musical history it is clear that not only is the artificial sharpening of the seventh of the scale so as to obtain a full close indefensible, but the perfect

---

[1] Contrast the two forms of the opening motif of Wagner's *Parsifal*.

H

cadence itself, where it can legitimately be had, is to be
avoided as much as possible in the harmonizing of plainsong,
and various forms of imperfect cadences are to be employed
as far as possible in its place, as being far more in keeping
with the melody.

After arguing so far for the safeguarding of the old
tonality in its purity a word must be added as to the safeguarding of the rhythm. For this end the accompaniment
should be reduced to a minimum. It should be small in
volume and very simple in texture, the parts moving as *little*
as possible and as small intervals as may be ; for every large
interval (more especially in the bass) tends to make it *sound*
heavy, and actually makes it difficult to avoid playing heavily,
thereby hampering the freedom of rhythm. We have most
of us heard plainsong so sung that it sounded like an elephant
waltzing : this is generally the fault of the accompaniment,
for, while the voices will, with very little encouragement, *if
practised without accompaniment,* learn to sing freely, to accompany them with equal delicacy is a work of intense difficulty.
It is the organ and the organist that ruin plainsong as a rule.
Even the most expert performer will do well to leave the
pedals almost entirely alone: even if played with the foot of
a fairy they would be generally too ponderous, in tone at any
rate if not in movement as well.

All the qualities necessary for good plainsong accompaniment can be summed up then in two words—it should be
diatonic[1] and unobtrusive.

In some kinds of plainsong—the simpler parts such as the
Tones and the Hymns—there is a real place for vocal
harmony, even though it is practically inevitable that the
rhythm should suffer from it to some extent. There should
be no doubt as to what that vocal harmony ought to be,
for the great polyphonic writers, Palestrina, Orlando di
Lasso, &c., have left masterpieces which all would do well

---

[1] This is of course not meant to exclude the transposition of any melody and its
accompaniment to any pitch which may be most suitable for performance.

to copy : unfortunately however most of the vocal harmonies at present in use are meretricious compositions in no particular style and quite unworthy of the place they hold.

But while the granting of a place to the laxer style of modal harmony for the purposes of *vocal* part writing may be defended on the ground of the perfection of the models left us in this style by Palestrina and his contemporaries, it cannot be too much insisted on that the proper style for plainsong accompaniment is the strict form of modal harmony. Anything else is in more or less degree a confusion of styles; and this is not a mere *doctrinaire* view, for in practice a simple accompaniment which is strictly diatonic and confined to the common chord and its inversions, will be found to be the best background to set off the ancient melodies both in their simple and in their elaborate forms.

MUSICAL EXAMPLES.

The Tones of the Psalms.

TONE 1

His is the in - to - na - tion of the First Tone,

(1)

and this is the me - di - a - tion : .. and this the end - ing.

(2)   (3)

... and this the end - ing.   ... and this the end - ing.

(4)   (5)

... and this the end - ing.   ... and this the end - ing.

(6)   (7)

... and this the end - ing.   ... and this the end - ing.

(8)   (9)

... and this the end - ing.   ... and this the end - ing.

Solemn form of Intonation, Mediation &c.
for *Benedictus* and *Magnificat*.

Bleff-ed be the Lord God of If- ra - el : for he hath vi- fi-ted &c
My foul   doth mag-ni- fy the Lord : and my   fpi-rit &c.

For remaining verfes fee p. 7

TONE II

His is the in - to - na - tion of the Se - cond Tone,

(1)

and this is the me- di - a - tion : ... and this the end - ing.

(2)

...and this the end - ing.

Solemn form of Intonation, Mediation &c.
for *Benedictus* and *Magnificat*.

Bleſſ-ed be the Lord God of Iſ- ra - el : for he hath vſ- ſi-ted &c.
Mÿ ſoul   doth mag-ni-fy the Lord : and my   ſpſ-rit &c.

For the remaining verſes ſee p. 8

TONE III

His is the in - to - na - tion of the Third Tone,

(1)

and this is the me- di - a - tion : ... and this the end - ing.

(2)   (3)

... and this the end-ing. ... and this the end - ing.

(3)

(4)   (5)

... and this the end- ing.   ... and this the end - ing.

(6)

... and this is the end-ing.

Intonation for Canticles.

Bleff - ed be &c.
My foul doth &c.

TONE IV

His is the in - to - na - tion of the Fourth Tone,

(1)

and this is the me - di - a - tion : ... and this is the end-ing.

(2)   (3)

... and this is the end - ing.   ... and this is the end - ing.

(4)   (5)

... and this is the end-ing.   ... and this is the end-ing.

(6)   (7)

... and this the end- ing.   ... and this the end- ing.

(4)

(8)   (9)

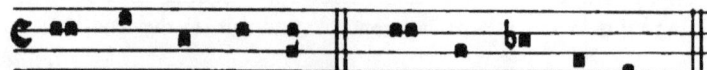

... and this the end- ing.   ... and this the end- ing.

Solemn form of Intonation & Mediation
for *Benedictus* and *Magnificat.*

Bleff - ed be the Lord God   of   If - ra - el :
My foul   doth mag - ni - fy the Lord :

For the remaining verses see p. 9

TONE V

His is the in - to - na - tion of the   Fifth   Tone,

(1)

and this is the me - di - a - tion : ... and this the end - ing.

(2)   (3)

... and this the end - ing.   ... and this the end - ing.

TONE VI

His is - the in - to - na - tion of the Sixth Tone,

and this is the me - di - a - tion : ... and this the end - ing.

(5)

Solemn form of Intonation, Mediation &c.
for *Benedictus* and *Magnificat*.

Bleſſ-ed be the Lord God of Iſ- ra - el : for he hath vi-ſi-ted &c.
My ſoul   doth mag- ni- fy the Lord : and my   ſpi-rit &c.

For remaining verſes ſee p. 7

TONE VII

His is the in - to - na-tion of the Se-venth Tone,

(1)

and this is the me- di - a - tion : ... and this the end - ing.

(2)   (3)

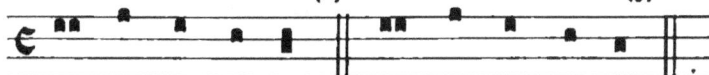

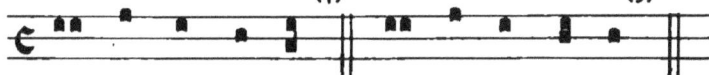

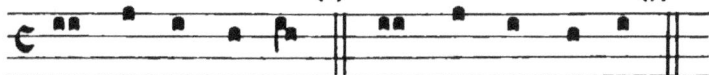

...and this the end - ing. ... and this the end - ing.

(4)   (5)

...and this the end-ing. ...and this the end - ing.

(6)   (7)

...and this the end-ing. ...and this the end - ing.

Intonation for Canticles.

Bleſſ- ed   be &c.
My ſoul doth &c.

Blessed be the Lord God of Is- ra- el : for he hath vi- si-ted &c.
My soul doth mag-ni- fy the Lord : and my spi-rit &c.

For remaining verses see p. 8

The Irregular or *Peregrine* Tone

His is the in-to-na-tion of the Ir- re- gu- lar Tone,

and this is the me- di- a - tion : ... and this the end-ing.

EXAMPLES OF THE ENDINGS

TONE I

(1)

(2)

(3)

(4)
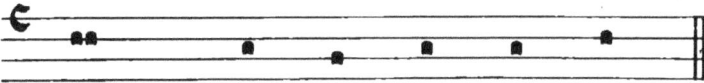

(5)

(6) and (7) are treated in a similar way.

(8)
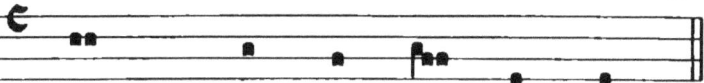

(9)

... with	hó-	ly	wor-	fhip.
... and	féa-	ther-	ed	fowls.
... a-	móng	thine	en-	e- mies.
... imá-	gine	a	vain	thing.
... togé-	ther	in	u-	ni- ty.
... his	näme....		pe-	rifh.
... to	täke......		a-	ny reft.
—	through	the	eaft	wind.
—	him	will	I	de- ftroy.
—	—	fhall	ferve	me
—	—	fhall	ne-	ver fall.
—	—	—	O	Chrift.
—	—	—	praife	the Lord.

ENDINGS *continued* :

TONE II (1)

TONE III (4)

(5)

	23			
.... with hó-	ly	wor-		fhip.
.... and féa-	ther-	ed		fowls.
.... amóng	thine	en-	e-	mies.
.... énemies	thy	foot-		ftool.
—	fhall	ferve		me.
—	fhall	ne-	ver	fall.
—	—	O		Chrift.
—	—	praife	the	Lord.

When the fyllable which receives the mufical accent is immediately preceded by another emphatic fyllable, the former of the two (diftinguifhed by the two dots placed above it) is reinforced by having the reciting-note added to the note to which it would ordinarily be fung : e.g.

TONE II (1)

TONE III (4)

(5)

	23			
.... his	nàme	pe-		rifh.
.... to	tàke	a-	ny	reft.

II. 2 *and* III. 1, 2 & 3, *follow the pointing of* Tone VI. *See p.* xiv.
For III. 6, *see pp.* xi. & xii. *under* Tone IV.

ENDINGS *continued* :

TONE IV (*a*) (*b*) (1)

(2) & (3) *are treated in a similar way.* (4)

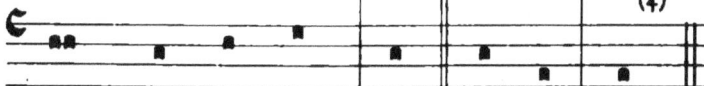

(5)

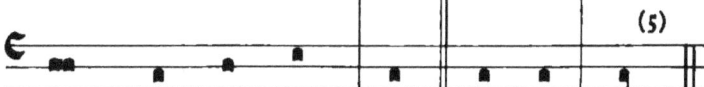

(8)

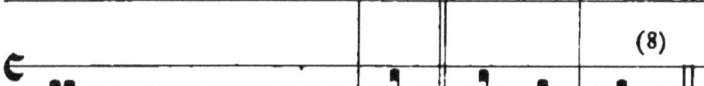

In (6) *the inflexion invariably falls on the* final *syllable; in* (7) *and* (9) *on the* penultimate *syllable.*

TONE III (6)

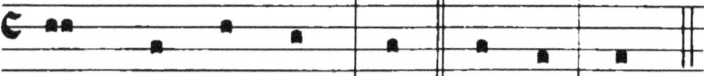

.... Lord	with	hó-	ly	wor-			ſhip.
.... midſt	a-	móng	thine		e -	ne-	mies.
.... i-	má-	gine	a	vain			thing.
.... to-	gé-	ther	in		u-	ni-	ty.
	ſhall	have	great	trou-			ble.
	and	to	the		ho-	ly	Ghoſt.
	—	through	the	eaſt			wind.
	—	him	will		I	de-	ſtroy.
	—	—	ſhall	ſerve			me.
	—.	—	ſhall		ne-	ver	fall.
	—	—	—	O			Chriſt.
	—	—	—			praiſe the	Lord.

In the above Table it will be ſeen that (a) illuſtrates the caſes where the accent falls on the penultimate *ſyllable, (b) where it occurs on the* antepenultimate.

(10)

EXAMPLES OF AMBROSIAN PSALM-TONES

EXAMPLES OF AMBROSIAN & GREGORIAN PSALMODY COMPARED

Mode i.

A

Po- su- é- runt su-per ca-put e- ius   cau-sam ip- sí-us scri-ptam,

G

A

Ie- sus Na- za- ré- nus,   rex Iu-de- ó- rum.   e u o u a e

G

Mode iii. (vi)

A

Be-ne-dí- ctus   dó-mi-nus De-us me-us.   e u o u a e

G

EXAMPLES OF ANTIPHONAL PSALMODY

Mode viii.

Ant. Ve-ní-te   a-do- ré- mus e - um : qui- a ip- se est dó-mi-nus

De- us nos-ter. *Ps.* Ve-ní- te exultémus dó-mi- no : iu- bi- lé-mus

De-o sa- lu- tá- ri nos-tro. Pre-oc-cupémus fáciem eius in confessi-

ó-ne : & in psalmis iubi- lé-mus e- i. *Ant.* Ve- ní- te &c.

Mode iv.

Ant. As-pér-ges me, Dó-mi-ne, hys-so-po, et mun-dá-bor :

la - vá- bis me, et su-pra ni-vem de-al- bá- bor. Ps: Mi-se-ré-re

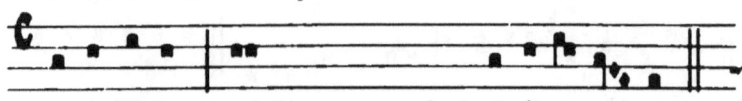

me- i, De-us : secúndum magnam miseri- cór-di-am tu - am.

As-pér-ges me &c.   Gló-ri- a Pa- tri et Fí- li- o,

et Spi- rí- tu- i San-cto. Si-cut erat . . . nunc et sem-per :

et in sécula se - cu- ló- rum, A - men. La- vá- bis me &c.

Mode ii.

Ant. Al-le-lu-ya,   Al-le-lu- ya,   Al-le- lu- ya,   Al - le- lu-ya.

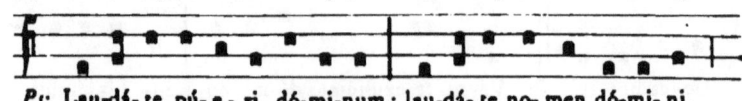

Ps: Lau-dá- te pú- e - ri dó-mi-num : lau-dá- te no- men dó-mi- ni,

Al- le- lu- ya.   Sit no-men &c.

Mode iv.

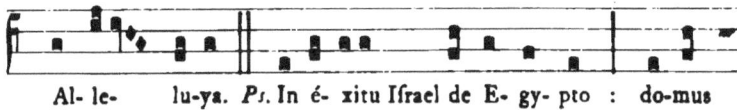

Al- le- lu-ya. *Ps.* In é- xitu Ifrael de E- gy- pto : do-mus

Iacob de pópu-lo bár-ba-ro, Al - le- lu-ya. Fa- ĉta eſt &c.

SPECIMEN OF PSALMODY FROM THE *Sarum Pſalter*, WITH ANTIPHONS

Ant. 1. O praiſe God in his ho- li-neſs. vi.

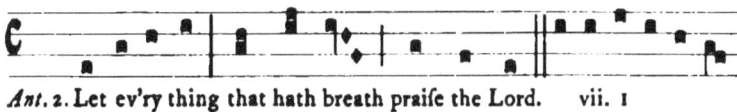

Ant. 2. Let ev'ry thing that hath breath praiſe the Lord. vii. 1

PSALM 150. *Laudate Dominum.*

O Praiſe God in his ho-li-neſs : praiſe him in the firma-ment
of his power.

2 Praiſe him in his no-ble aĉts : praiſe him according to his
ex-cel-lent greatneſs.

3 Praiſe him in the ſound of the trum-pet : praiſe him up-on
the lute and harp.

4 Praiſe him in the cym-bals and dan-ces : praiſe him up- on the
ſtrings and pipe.

5 Praiſe him upon the well-tu-ned cym-bals : praiſe him up-on
the loüd cymbals.

6 Let every thing that hath breath : — — — praiſe the Lord.
Glory be to the Fa-ther, and to the Son : and to the holy Ghoſt.
As it was in the beginning, is now, and ev-er ſhall be : world
with-out end. Amen.

EXAMPLES OF THE POINTING OF LATIN & ENGLISH COMPARED

Mediations

3

7

.... le - tá - bi - tur rex. Qui fa - cit hæc. Di - lé - xi.
.... et é - ri - pe me. Lord, lift thou up. This I had.
.... thy júdg- ments are right.
.... and fá - fhion- ed me.

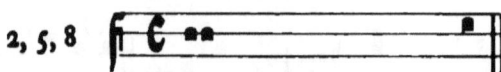

2, 5, 8

4

.... meó- rum quís eft :
... auxíli- um abs te :
.... con - trí - tus eft :
.... in E phrá - ta :
... proceed a- gainft him :
.... con- cér - ning me :
.... feet like hárts' feet :

Endings

5 4

7 6

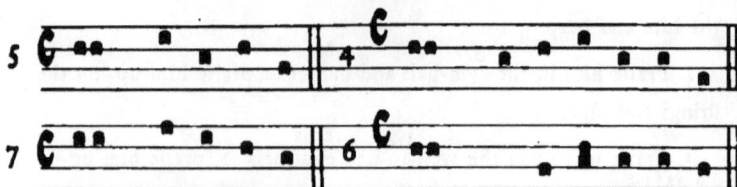

... conver-tún-tur ad cor.
... vi- ví - fi - ca me.
... robo-rá - bi- tur vir.
... re-fréfh-ea my foul.
... the in- no- cent blood.

8

... fru- mén- ti fá- ti- at te.
... quó- ni- am hó- mi- nes funt.
... my fáce hath có- ver- ed me.
... that he bild the Cá-tho-lick faith.

ALMA REDEMPTORIS

Mode v (transposed)

Al - - - - - - - - - ma Re- dem- ptó- ris Ma- ter, que pér-

vi- a ce- li Por- ta ma- nes, et stel- la ma- ris,

suc-cúr-re ca -dén- ti, Súr-ge-re qui cu- rat pó-pu-lo. Tu que

ge- nu- í- sti, Na-tú- ra mi-rán- te, tu-um san-ctum

Ge- ni- tó- rem, Vir- go pri- us ac po-sté- ri- us, Ga-

bri- é- lis ab o- re Su-mens il- lud A-ve, pec-ca-tó-

rum mi-se- ré- re. e u o u a e

(16)

Types of the Modes

Primum quærite re-gnum De-i.

Se-cundum au-tem si-mi-le est hu- ic.

Ter-ti-a di-es est quod hæc fac-ta sunt.

Quar-ta vi-gi- li-a ve-nit ad e- os.

Quinque prudentes intraverunt ad nupti-as.

Sexta ho- ra se-dit su-per pu-te- um

Septem sunt spi-ri-tus ante thronum De-i.

Octo sunt be-a- ti- tu- di-nes.

PLAINSONG HYMN MELODIES

HYMNS OF THE LITTLE HOURS

1 AT PRIME   H. 152   A.& M. 1   Ferial   Mode viii

Now that the day-light fills the sky, We lift our hearts to God on high;

That He in all we do or say, Would keep us free from harm to-day.

2   Christmas & Epiphany Eves, &c.   Mode ii

3   Christmas Day, All Saints & Dedication festivals   Mode iii

4   In the Dedication Octave   Mode vi

¶ *For references to the melodies used at other seasons, see the Index.*

5 At Trace   H. 153   A. & M. 9   On greater festivals   Mode iv

Come Ho-ly Ghost with God the Son, And God the Fa-ther ev-er One;

Shed forth Thy grace with-in our breast, And dwell with us a rea-dy guest.

6 On Sundays & lesser festivals   Mode iv

7 Ferial   Mode viii

8 In Whitsun Week   H. 154   A. & M. 157   Mode viii

Come, Ho-ly Ghost, Cre-a-tor blest, Vouchsafe within our souls to rest ;

Come with Thy grace & heav'nly aid, & fill the hearts which Thou hast made.

9 At Sext H. 155 A. & M. 10 On greater festivals Mode ii

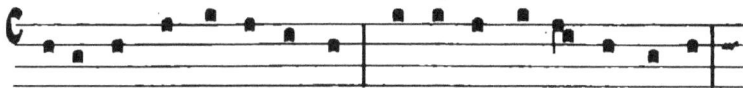

O God of truth, O Lord of might, Who ord'rest time & change a-right

And send'st the early morning ray, And light'st the glow of per-fect day

10 On Sundays and lesser festivals Mode ii

At None H. 156 A.& M. 11
On greater festivals as at Sext. (Melody 9.)
On lesser festivals and ferial as at Terce. (Melodies 6 & 7.)

11 At Compline Ferial H. 157 A.& M. 15 Mode viii

To Thee be-fore the close of day, Cre-a-tor of the world, we pray That

with Thy wont-ed fa-vour Thou Would'st be our Guard & Keep-er now.

12 In Lent till Passion-tide H. 159 A.& M. 95 Mode ii

O Christ, Who art the light & day, Thy beams chase night's dark shades away:

The very Light of Light we own Who hast Thy glorious light made known.

13 In Passion-tide   H. 160   A. & M. 493   Mode viii

Ser-vant of God, re- mem- ber   The hal-lowed Font's be-dew-ing,

The Seal of Con- fir- ma- tion,   Thine in- ner man re- new-ing.

14 In Easter-tide   H. 161   A.& M. 141   Mode viii

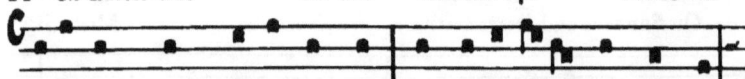

Jesu, Who brought'st redemption nigh, Word of the Father, God most high :

O Light of Light, to man unknown, And watchful Guardian of Thine own.

HYMNS OF THE FERIAL SEASONS

15 Sunday Mattins   Epiphany-tide   H. 23   Mode iv

On this the day that saw the earth From ut- ter dark-ness first have birth,

The day its Maker rose a-gain, And vanquish'd death, and burst our chain.

16 Sunday Mattins   Trinity-tide   H. 83   Mode vi

Now from the slum-bers of the night a- ri-sing, Chant we the Psal-mist's

ho-ly me- di-ta-tions, And with new fer-vour raise to God Almighty

Hymns of de-vo-tion.   A- men.

(21)

Sundays in Advent

Salus eterna

Mode vii

SA - viour e- ter- nal! Health and life of the world un- fail- ing ;)
Light ev-er-last-ing,   and in ve- ri-ty our re-demp-tion : }

Griev-ing that the a- ges   of men must per- ish through the temp-
Still in heav'n a- bi-ding, Thou cam- est earth-ward of Thine own

ter's wi- li- ness,) Then free- ly and gra-cious-ly deign-ing to
great cle-men-cy: } To   lost ones and per-ish- ing gav - est Thou

as- sume hu-ma-ni- ty, } Fill-ing all the world with joy.
Thy free de - li - ver-ance, }

O Christ, our souls and bo- dies cleanse by Thy per- fect sa - cri-fice:)
So we,   as tem-ples pure and bright, fit for Thine a- bode may be. }

By Thy for-mer Ad- vent jus-ti- fy:) That when in a blaze of glo-ry
By Thy se-cond grant us li- ber-ty: }

Thou de-scend-est, Judge of all ; Robed in rai-ment un-de-fi-led, we

may shine, and ev- er fol-low, Lord, Thy foot-steps blest where-e'er

they lead us.

Laudes Deo Devotas

A Sequence for Whitsuntide

SING to God your prai- ses high, Voice and heart both mu- sic
Ci - ti - zens of hea- ven's

ma-king, } For the Ho-ly Spi- rit's grace up- on this day light-ed
king-dom. { in tongues of fire out of

on th' A-pos-tles, } Now may the heavenly Pa-ra-clete a - bi - ding
heav'n de-scend-ing. { and make us

in us wash out our of - fen - ces, } May He with- in our
tem-ples meet for his in-dwell- ing. {

bo-soms place rich store of His gifts and gra- ces to aid us, }
that we may con-form our life to His bid-ding. {

So thro' the a- ges of a- ges } To God be all praise and
We may pro-claim Al- le- lu- ya. {

pow- er and hon- our and glo- ry.

Festivals of our Lady

Missus Gabriel de celis

G A-briel, from the heav'n de- scen-ding, On the faith-ful Word at-
That good word and sweet he pligh-teth In the bo- som where it

ten- ding, Is in ho-ly con-verse blen-ding With the Vir-gin full
ligh-teth, And for *E-va A- ve* wri- teth, Chan-ging E- va's name

of grace : ⎫ At the pro-mise that he sen-deth God th'In-car-nate
& race. ⎭ She, with-out a fa-ther, bear-eth, She no bri-dal

Word de- scen-deth ; Yet no car- nal touch of-fen-deth Her, the un-
u- nion sha- reth, And a pain-less birth de- cla-reth That she bare

de- fi- led one. ⎫ Tale that won-d'ring search en- ti- ces ! But be-
the Roy-al Son. ⎭ High the sign, its place as- su-ming In the

lieve—& that suf-fi- ces ; It is not for man's de-vi- ces Here
bush, the un-con-su-ming ; Mor-tal, veil thine eyes pre-su-ming, Loose

to pry with gaze un-meet : ⎫ As the rod by won-drous pow-er,
thy shoes from off thy feet. ⎭ Hail the Fruit, O world, with glad-ness !

Mois-ten'd not by dew or show-er, Bare the al-mond and the flow-er,
Fruit of joy & not of sad-ness: A-dam had not laps'd to mad-ness

Thus he came, the Vir-gin's Fruit : { Je-sus kind a-bove all o-ther,
had he tas-ted of its shoot. { He once cra-dled in a man-ger,

Gen-tle Child of gen-tle mo-ther, In the sta-ble born our Bro-ther,
Heal our sin & calm our dan-ger ; For our life, to this world stran-ger,

Whom th'an-ge-lic hosts a-dore ;
Is in pe-ril ev-er-more.

EXAMPLES OF THE PSALMODY OF THE TRACTS

Intonation *Recitation* *Inflection*

et	Æ- di-	fi-	ca-	vit	tur-rim in	me-	di-	o	e-	jus
et	vo- lun-ta-	te	la-			bi-	o-	rum	c-	jus
	ho- no- ri-	fi-	ca-	tus et	e- quum et		a-	scen-	so-	tem
	et ju-		sti-				ti-	a	e-	jus
	nos au-	tem	po-	nim	Do- mi-	ni	pu-	lus	c-	jus
	vi- ne-	a	c-				ni	Sa-	ba-	oth

KYRIE. *Rex Splendens*, from 11th Century Troper.

Plainsong

Harmony

Ky - ri - e - . . . . . . ley - son.

PART OF A GRADUAL

PART OF A GRADUAL

GREGORIAN VERSION

Jus-tus ut palma flo- re- bit : si-cut ce- drus

A summo cœ- lo e- gres- si- o

Tol- li- te por- tas prin- ci- pes

Li- ba- ni e- jus : et oc-cur-sus e- jus

ves- tras : et e-le- va- mi-ni por- tæ

us-que ad sum- mum e- jus

æ - ter-na - les et in-tro-i

bit Rex

glo - ri - a.

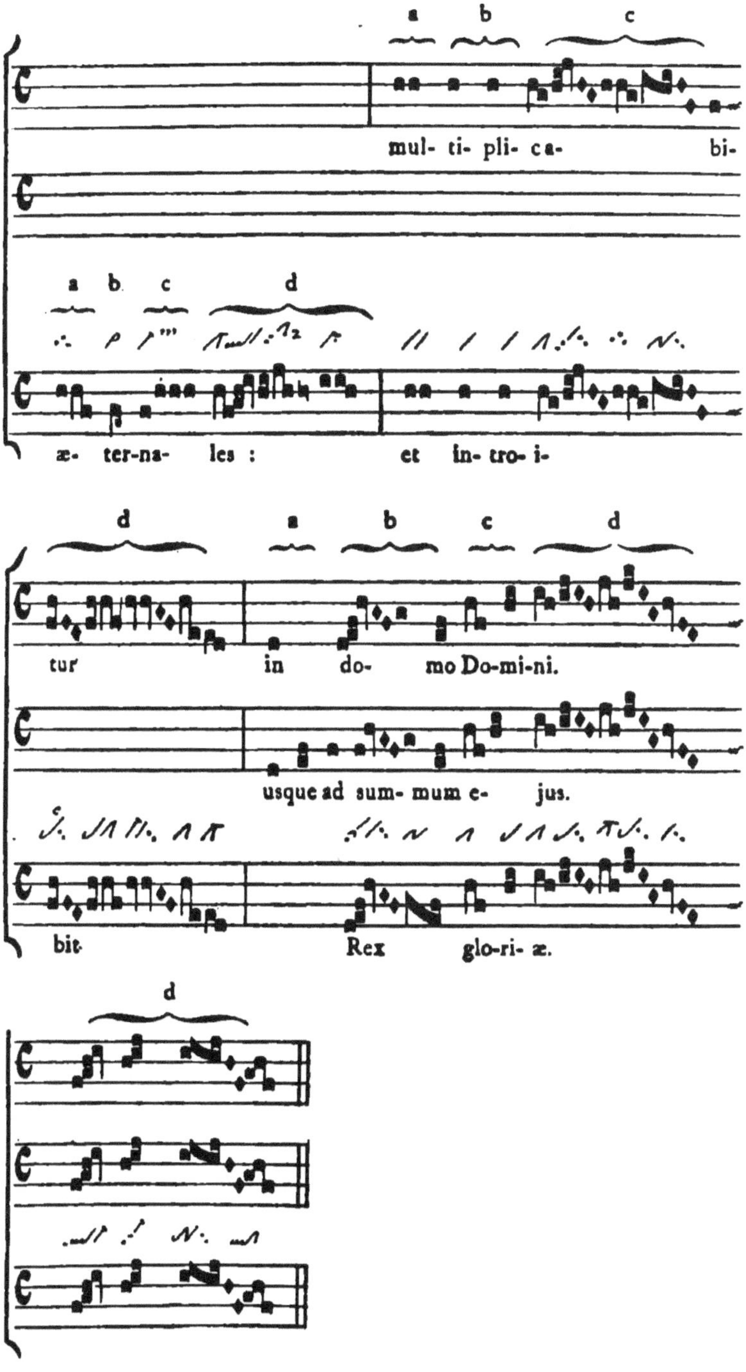
a b c
mul- ti- pli- ca- bi-
a b c d
æ- ter-na- les : et in- tro- i-
d a b c d
tur in do- mo Do-mi-ni.
usque ad sum- mum e- jus.
bit. Rex glo-ri- æ.
d

www.ingramcontent.com/pod-product-compliance
Lightning Source LLC
Chambersburg PA
CBHW030614270326
41927CB00007B/1170